BABA

May I Answer

By the same author

Shirdi Sai Baba and other Perfect Masters

श्री शिरडी साई बाबा एवं अन्य सद्गुरु

साई शरण में

BABA

May I Answer

C. B. Satpathy

Sterling Paperbacks

STERLING PAPERBACKS
An imprint of
Sterling Publishers (P) Ltd.
A-59, Okhla Industrial Area, Phase-II,
New Delhi-110020.
Tel: 26387070, 26386209; Fax: 91-11-26383788
E-mail: mail@sterlingpublishers.com
ghai@nde.vsnl.net.in
www.sterlingpublishers.com

BABA May I Answer
© 2009, C. B. Satpathy
ISBN 978 81 207 4594 0

Printed in India
Printed and Published by Sterling Publishers Pvt. Ltd.,
New Delhi-110 020.

Dedicated to

Spiritual Seekers
and
Baba's Devotees

We should always strive to elevate our consciousness to a purer state. *If we really want to have a direct vision or experience of the universal form of God, then we have to clean the old memories, experiences, thoughts and convictions from our mental storehouse. Otherwise, in place of universality, limited and distorted pictures will be painted by negative and non creative thoughts in our mind.*

Foreword

By the grace of Sai Baba, I had the privilege of going through the manuscript of the new book *MAY I ANSWER*. The questions asked under 22 broad themes centre around the Sadguru Shri Sai Baba. The enquiries appear to be very spontaneous and natural coming from people who are a part of the ever increasing Sai following. The answers given by Shri C.B. Satpathy have been equally spontaneous and natural. A very ardent devotee of Shri Shirdi Sai Baba, Shri Satpathy has been working unceasingly for last 18 years, trying to bring Sai teachings to the people with utmost clarity and simplicity. The answers on various topics have been given with as much scientific and rational explanation as possible keeping in view the thought processes of the new generation of young people in different parts of the world. In this process, however, emotive contents have not been neglected. I think that such a natural style of answering is possible only from an Ankit Santan (chosen child) of Sai Baba. It is as if the Sadguru (Perfect Master), Shri Shirdi Sai Baba is responding to questions from devotees and persons with a spiritual quest.

I have thoroughly enjoyed going through the manuscript and felt spiritual exhilaration. I hope the readers of the publication will be blessed by Shri Sai Baba to follow the spiritual path shown by Him.

Population Foundation of India   **A R Nanda I.A.S. (R)**
B-28 Qutab Institutional Area
New Delhi – 110 016

The Guru is always hidden in the disciple. When the worldly covers are taken out and the mind is purified then the real image of the Guru is reflected in the disciple. There is no difference between the disciple and the Guru as they live in each other in a subtle form.

Preface

The spread of the name and fame of Shri Sai Baba of Shirdi within the last two decades is a phenomenon by itself. From 1999 onwards a number of websites were created in the name of Baba, the world over. One of the main sites was created by Shri Mukund Raj, a prominent Sai devotee from Chicago, U.S. I visited Chicago to inaugurate the Sai Utsav-2000 in the month of November. There was a large conglomeration of Sai devotees and others, more than two thousand in number, including hundreds of families from U.S., Canada, UK and some other Latin American countries. By the grace of Baba, I addressed the huge gathering of Sai devotees from various countries and followers of other paths and religions on the life and preachings of Baba for three days. This event created an effective world forum of Sai devotees to share their thoughts on Shri Sai Baba of Shirdi and other related matters. It was later followed by similar Sai Utsav events at Sydney, Australia during winter in 2001 and at Johannesburg and Nairobi in Africa during winter of 2003.

Following these world Sai conferences I started receiving a large number of questions regarding Sai Baba of Shirdi through the websites, not only from His devotees but also from people with a religious bent of mind. They were too numerous to answer but nevertheless I tried to satisfy the devotees considering it to be a job done in the service of Baba. Some of the questions were limited to the specific thoughts of a devotee but a majority of them were generic in nature. Given this situation, it was felt necessary to bring out a publication in the form of a compendium of these questions and answers.

Messages circulated on various occasions between 2004 and 2009 through different magazines and websites are also compiled herewith.

This book has been substantially amended and updated with lots of new questions that the devotees have asked and my answers thereof. The name and fame of Shri Shirdi Sai Baba has expanded immensely during the last decade. More than a thousand temples have come up in His name in India and abroad. Shri Shirdi Sai Baba has become a household name in India. The devotees' urge to know more and more about the Master is clearly discernable from the never-ending series of questions they put through different mediums. I hope that my answers to their queries will benefit them.

By this time, an ardent Sai devotee named Shri Ravi Mehra had shifted to U.S.A. from Noida on a job. Ravi used to visit me frequently when he was in India and suggested that we should bring this out as an in-house publication. An in house publication captioned "May I answer" was published in the year 2001 A.D.

I thank Mukund Raj and Ravi Mehra for the immense help they have rendered to me in publication of this book. I thank Ms Shipra Shukla for assisting me painstakingly in the compilation and correction of the manuscript. My special thanks to Shri A. R. Nanda, IAS (Retd), an ardent Sai devotee, for manuscript corrections and writing a foreword to this book. At the end I thank Shri S. K. Ghai of Sterling Publishers Pvt. Ltd. for the publication of this book.

May Shri Sai Baba bless us all to follow the path shown by Him.

Delhi   **C. B. Satpathy**
Ram Navami 3rd April, 2009
E-mail: mayianswer@gmail.com

Contents

SECTION II : MESSAGES

SECTION I : MAY I ANSWER

The ongoing experience of human souls, life after life, is to experience that timeless reality which we call God. Only the compassion of the Perfect Master can evolve us to experience such a reality. Therefore, we should always pray to Sai Baba, the Incarnation of the Age to show and lead us in that path.

Original painting of Baba by Shri Shyamrao Jaiker

SHIRDI SAI BABA AND SADGURUS
(PERFECT MASTERS)

Shirdi Sai Baba and Sadgurus (Perfect Masters)

Who is Shirdi Sai Baba? Why is He named like this?

The childhood or the parent given name of the Saint you are referring to is unknown. He is called by different names such as Shirdi Sai Baba or Sai Baba of Shirdi or Sainath Maharaj or Sairam etc. He was a Sadguru of a very high spiritual stage who finally settled at Shirdi for about sixty years before entering into His Maha Samadhi on, 15th October 1918. Presently Shirdi is a village in the district Ahmadnagar in the state of Maharashtra, India. Most of His spiritual, religious, social and philanthropic activities that made Him known all over the country were during the period of His stay at Shirdi for about sixty years. Therefore He is popularly known as Shirdi Sai Baba.

What does this word *Sai mean*? I have heard of it in different contexts and am confused?

This word is used in most of the Indian languages like Hindi, Urdu, Punjabi, Oriya, Marathi etc. The word Sai means a protector, God, a Spiritual Master, a religious teacher, a ruler, a king, a powerful man or a father, husband and even lover.

Was Shirdi Sai Baba a *Sadguru* or an *Avatar?* Can you please explain?

Before one should ask whether Shirdi Sai Baba is an *Avatar* or a *Sadguru* one must know the difference between the two. A Sadguru is one who dispels ignorance and lights wisdom and guides the devotees towards the Path of God. An *Avatar* is one (none else but God Himself) who descends in a human body to uplift mankind. He can incarnate as a full *Avatar* that is, with all the 16 *kalas (sixteen types of powers)* or as a partial *Avatar* to establish Dharma (with a few *kalas* out of this 16). I firmly believe that Shri Shirdi Sai Baba is an *Avatar* of God. The Lord in His form has descended in order to uplift mankind and re-establish *dharma*. He always used to act as if He was just a fakir and a servant of God but many a times in front of devotees when He was in a spiritually ecstatic mood, He declared that He was the Lord Himself. The qualities required to call Him an *Avatar* are Omnipotence, Omnipresence and Omniscience. He had full control over all the five elements (Panchatattwa). We all know that He controlled the fire and rain as narrated in chapter 11 of "Shri Sai Satcharitra", the life story of Shri Sainath. It is seen that usually a religion or path that is established by an Avatar goes on expanding for hundreds of years ever after His Samadhi. The phenomenal expansion of the Sai movement in India and abroad is a clear indication about the spiritual status of Shri Sai Baba of Shirdi.

Many devotees address Baba by different names like Baba, Sai Baba, Sai Ram, Sai Nath. By which name should I call Him?

You can call Him by any of the names. We have Vishnu Sahasra Naam depicting various attributes of Lord Vishnu. Similarly devotees have a tendency of creating newer and newer names for the Master out of sheer love. Lord Shri Krishna had so many names. However, it is the last name which appeals to our heart the most. Any name of Baba which spontaneously appeals to your mind and soul should be used.

Why did Sai refer to the Masjid, sometimes as Masjid Mayee and sometimes as Dwarka Mayee? What does Dwarkamayee signify?

Dwaraka was the capital of Lord Krishna. It was also called 'Dwarawati'. Lord Krishna created Dwaraka (presently in Gujarat) for the final habitation of the Yadava family (His clan) and security from attackers like Jarasandha and others. Like a mother protecting a child, Dwaraka, protected the Yadavas. Baba has given the same concept to the dilapidated mosque where He stayed for over 60 years. He gave love, protection and solution to the problems of His devotees. Baba has been quoted saying in "Shri Sai Satcharitra" that

Dwarakamayee protects its children i.e. His devotees. The word 'Mayee' in Hindi means mother.

I am always imagining about Sai Baba, but I do not know how He looked like. Please can you tell me how he looked like?

A few photographs of Baba and the paintings (particularly those by Jayakar who had painted Baba in real life) and others give some idea of how He looked like. During His first visit to Shirdi in the in the fifth decade of the nineteenth century, He had curly hair, golden hue in His well formed and sportsman like body. His height was about 5 feet 8 inches or above. His feet and hands were longer than His body. His eyes had bluish tinge. Later He became bald. He always sported a thick mustache and got His beard trimmed. He had a powerful but kind look. His gazes were piercing as if He could read the mind. (**For more details please read the article "What Baba Looked Like" in the book "Shirdi Sai Baba and other Perfect Masters".**)

What is the relevance of Sai's teachings in today's world?

Although volumes can be written on His magnanimous personality yet the most important preachings of Sai Baba of Shirdi that are relevant in today's world are: -

Love towards all including animals, birds and insects: Baba used to feed dogs even before He partook of His meals. He had equal sympathy for His horse Shyamkarna and other animals around Him at Shirdi. He extended His love even to a useless rock which He used for washing clothes or at times used to sit on it. Today that rock can be seen in Dwarkamai and is worshipped by devotees who come there. To a great extent devotees are following such preachings of Baba. People are seen distributing clothes, food, etc. to the poor. *Narayana seva* is going on all over the world in various Sai centers.

Religious tolerance: Shirdi Sai Baba looked after the Hindus, Muslims, Parsees equally. We can find people of all religions visiting His Samadhi temple even now. He always believed in the peaceful co-existence of all species. In today's world there is a lot of intolerance among the people of various religions and sects. People must believe that all human faiths may be different but the goal is one. Shirdi Sai devotees are equal before God. At Baba's time Muslims, Hindus, Sikhs, Parsees and Christians, etc. used to share their views and talk with each other like real brothers in Shirdi. They firmly believe that flowers may be many but the God to whom the flowers are offered is one. Stars may be many but light is one. Similarly paths may be different but the goal is the same.

Social Harmony: Shirdi Sai never allowed people to have ill feelings towards each other on the basis of social differentiations as caste, creed etc. People of all religions and castes used to have food together, sleep together, hug each other and share Hukka. When they felt loathsome to do the same He castigated them and told them everything is *Atma*. If they hated them then they are in fact hating Him who is residing in them. People who believe in Baba should follow the same thing. Treat all mankind as brothers and live happily. Believe in brotherhood of mankind under the fatherhood of God.

My mummy and papa are very fond of Baba. Through them I have developed some love for Baba. But does He love children as parents do?

At Shirdi, Baba was very fond of children. Most of the children at Shirdi used to go to Baba and get sweetmeats. Some children used to get money from Him. Baba always forbade the elder persons or the parents to ill treat or beat the children. Once when Shyama, chased his son Uddhav, the child ran to Baba and took shelter behind Him. Baba told Shyama that his son will henceforth, not go to the school but will serve Him (Baba) throughout his life. This is exactly what happened in the life of Uddhav. Baba's promise to protect and guide His devotees even after leaving His mortal body includes children.

I am coming from Toronto and want to visit Shirdi. Can you tell me when and how to go to Shirdi?

One can go to Shirdi whenever one wishes to. Since you would be reaching India on an overseas travel, it is better that you take atleast a day's rest at Mumbai or Delhi or wherever your aircraft lands before proceeding to Shirdi. If you proceed straight to Shirdi which is about 6 ½ hrs journey from Mumbai, 4 hrs from Pune, 2 ½ hrs from

Aurangabad or 2 hrs from Nasik by road; or by train you will suffer from jet lag and will not be able to easily partake of the numerous devotional activities including the four Aartis that take place on a daily basis at Shirdi. When approaching the shrine or the Samadhi, one should be in a peaceful and happy state of mind.

What are the activities that I should do in a limited time of one or two days of stay in Shirdi?

Usually whenever devotees used to visit Shirdi at the time of Baba or even today they get into a series of activities and get less time to sleep. The pleasant atmosphere of festivity at Shirdi from early morning, about 4 am to midnight about 12 pm keeps them fully occupied. Some people visiting Shirdi, even spend the whole night meditating on Baba. You should definitely attend the four aratis (Kakad arati 4:30 am, Madhyan Arati 12:00, Dhoop Arati at sunset, Sheja Arati at 10:30 pm). Visit the Samadhi Mandir, Dwarkamayi Masjid, Chavadi, Gurusthan, Khandoba mandir, Hanuman mandir, Lendi Bagh, Nandadeep, Shani mandir, Ganpati mandir and meditation hall of the Sansthan. One should offer Chaddar, Coconut, Prashad etc. at the Samadhi Mandir, Dwarkamayi and at other places. One can also purchase books, magazines, photographs and audio-video materials on Baba as they are available in plenty for future use and distribution. They can even read 'Shri Sai Satcharitra' in the parayan kakshya.

Recently I received 'Shri Sai Satcharitra' book from a devotee of Sai Baba. Although I have visited Shirdi but, I have not read this book. Can you tell me the significance of Shri Sai Satcharitra?

The significance of 'Shri Sai Satcharitra' is:
- This is the first and foremost book based on the life-story of Shri Sai Baba, which was originally composed in Marathi verse form. The writing of the book started in the lifetime of Baba with His blessings. It is like a standard text for all Sai devotees.
- The Hindi translation of this book is in simple Hindi language, which can be understood even by a common man.

- The divine truth imparted by this book is even greater than the knowledge contained in the Vedas and Geeta, because all the characters and events in it are real and authentic as also recorded in details by many devotees.

- Because of the expression in simple Hindi it is easy for everyone to comprehend it. Had it been written in Sanskrit it would have been difficult for most of the people to understand it. Today there are very few people who can understand Sanskrit language properly and absorb the meaning and substance easily.

- The spiritual essence contained in all the religious scriptures like Vedas, Geeta, Yoga Vashisht is found in the life-story of Shri Sainath.

- The concepts on God and spirituality are explained in such a simple yet comprehensive manner in 'Shri Sai Satcharitra' that no additional book or commentary etc. is required to understand it. It has a natural flow so the readers start feeling as if they had been closely associated with the events described in it, in their past life.

- I may mention here that the glory of Shri Sai is spreading in the world, far and wide, in such an amazing way that detailed information about Shri Sai and 'Shri Sai Satcharitra' is available in various websites on the Internet for interested readers.

- The foremost duty of a Sai devotee is therefore to read 'Shri Sai Satcharitra' and absorb it by heart if possible. The more they read this book, the more it will bring them closer to Baba and all their doubts and apprehensions will be cleared.

- It also has been experienced that during a crisis, if any devotee is searching for an answer and randomly opens 'Shri Sai Satcharitra' praying Baba sincerely and with faith, his answer can be found in that open page.

- Many people have got their desired benefits after reading 'Shri Sai Satcharitra' for a week or so in a parayana form.

Can I tell my friends, who are also Sai devotees to go through 'Shri Sai Satcharitra' book? In what manner can this book be best utilized by the Sai devotees and others?

'Shri Sai Satcharitra' can be utilized by all Sai devotees in the following manner:

1. Get the book, 'Shri Sai Satcharitra' in whatever language one chooses to read as translated versions are available in the market in most of the Indian languages. Neatly wrap it up in a piece of new cloth, and place it near Baba's statue or Pooja place with due sanctity.

2. Whether at home or elsewhere, one should always try to read a few pages of the book every night before going to sleep. Every devotee should try to keep Baba as the last thought in mind before entering into sleep.

3. During crisis or in order to get rid of any serious problem(s) one should read devotionally for a week in the form of 'Parayana', as is mentioned in 'Shri Sai Satcharitra'. If possible, such Parayana should begin on a Thursday or on some other special day, such as Ramnavami, Dussehra, Gurupurnima, Janmashtmi, Mahashivratri, Navratri, etc. After its completion on the seventh day one should feed the poor and destitute either in the temple/ home or wherever possible.

4. One should read it sitting in some isolated corner in the temple or in front of Baba's statue or Photograph/painting. If other people are present, then it can be read out to them or with them as well. Group reading should always be encouraged.

5. Wherever and whenever possible, it should be read continuously from sunrise to sunset in the temples on auspicious days. Devotees may be asked to read it by turn as is done in the case of chanting of the holy name i.e. Naamjap. Encourage children to read this book. Question answer competition from the "Shri Sai Satcharitra" can be organized in temples and other suitable places.

6. 'Shri Sai Satcharitra' should be read to the devotees - sick, old aged and those nearing death as much as possible. They will surely get peace and blessings of Baba.

7. 'Shri Sai Satcharitra' is a reasonably priced book and is easily available at Shirdi. Therefore, any devotee visiting Shirdi must bring a few copies with him to distribute among the deserving people free of cost.

8. At times, of distress and agony if one will sincerely search for
    answers from 'Shri Sai Satcharitra' he will not only find the
    answers but also solace. Consequently his faith will grow in Baba.
    I pray Shri Sainath to reveal the divine knowledge and mysteries
    contained in this book to the devotees in the same manner in
    which he had inspired Hemandpant to write this book sitting in
    his heart. Shri Sai Satcharitra should be taken by all Sai devotees
    with as much seriousness as one takes Geeta or Bible.

**Like my neighbor, who is a genuine devotee of Baba; I want to
do one *week parayana* of Shri Sai Satcharitra. Kindly tell me
how to go about it?**

Before doing 'parayana' you must understand what the word parayana
means. In short, parayana means promising to oneself to complete
reading of a religious book or a part thereof or Pooja or recitation of
a mantra within a certain period of time. In your case you want to do
parayana of Shri Sai Satcharitra that means going through the entire
book word by word and page by page and complete the reading by
the seventh day from the day of beginning to read it. A parayana is
not a quick reading for the sake of reading only or an overview while
turning over the pages or reading a few portions as per one's taste and
leaving the other portions. Parayana is not starting of reading anywhere
in the middle of the book and ending anywhere. During the time of
Baba, He prescribed completion of the reading of religious scriptures
written by Sant Gyaneshwar, Tukaram etc. to devotees. Most of these
pothis were read by the devotees on the orders of Baba at a place
known as "Dixit Wada" named so, as it was built by Kaka Saheb
Dixit.

If possible, reading of the 'Pothi' as parayana should begin on a
Thursday or on any other special day, such as Ramnavami, Dussehra,
Gurupurnima, Janmashtmi, Mahashivratri, Navratri, etc. The Shri
Sai Satcharitra book is apportioned in seven parts for the purpose of
parayana in seven days time. You will do well to follow the instructions
regarding the parayana given in the Shri Sai Satcharitra. On
completion of parayana you may like to feed the poor people or make
a donation to an institution working for the poor people.

I find nowadays gold being donated liberally for Baba's Mukhut, or for his seat, with crores of rupees being the spent for the same. During his lifetime, Baba never wanted any of these, and even when he was being led to the Chavadi during the evenings every alternate day, He would protest, saying, "Bhau. Why all this. I have nothing except a tin pot and a chillum, and am a poor fakir. Don't get these attachments to me." In such a condition, is it right for us to do what we are doing, even if the donor wants it done. Cannot this be used for helping needy students in their education, or making available better hospital facilities? Or even undertaking poor feeding? I am aware these activities are there, but what there is can be improved upon rather than do what we are doing, which Gurudev never liked.

When Baba was in Shirdi, all types of people the rich and the poor used to visit Him. They used to offer Him whatever they could offer like coconut, sweets, garland, flower, coins, silver and gold etc. Baba is 'Nirguna' which means He is beyond the attraction of any of these materials. He used to accept whatever the devotees gave. The rich ones used to give gold and silver and the poor used to give coconut or sweets and coins. His love was there for all and equally. Therefore, it does not matter what metal is used in relation to Baba.

Baba is said to be a Sadguru. What does it mean?

Sadgurus are spiritual personalities holding human form who are in pure divine state of self realisation. They possess all the attributes and powers of God in themselves. Vasudev Shri Krishna was God Incarnate, who had assumed a human body. What is Sai Baba in reality? Without the direct experience of Baba no one can infer anything merely through the aid of his imagination and emotions. When you will have the direct experience of the true form of Baba you will know. But it is for sure that Baba was in a *paramukta* state (fully liberated soul) and was beyond the cycle of birth and death through which all mortals travel. He had divine powers to control elements of nature and lives of millions of people at His will. There is plenty of literature available on Him which establishes His omnipotence, omniscience and omnipresence.

What is the role of a *Sadguru* like Baba in our life?

The *Sadguru* gives the ability of God realization to the deserving human beings. His first function is to evolve them, stage by stage and give the experience of attaining the state of '*Paramhamsa*' to the very, very few deserving human beings. Without the grace of a Sadguru it is impossible to achieve this state. One in billions can achieve this '*Paramhamsa*' or 'Sadguru' state. '*Paramukti*' and '*turiyavastha*' can be attained with great difficulty.

The *Sadguru* removes all the impediments in the path of spiritual evolution of any human being who comes in contact with Him in any way. *Sadguru* breaks the wrong and illusory concepts (*maya*) of a devotee collected through a few lives of his existence. All human concepts are relative and illusory in nature. When ignorance is dispelled by the Guru the disciple's inner knowledge gets illuminated itself. The true knowledge is veiled by various concepts taught to us from childhood and experience acquired by us. Therefore, it is necessary to shed them before the mind is free to accept new and truthful concepts. For a man who thinks that he is the most intelligent person, the *Sadguru* wipes out his ego of intellect till he realises that his intellect was full of follies. The *Sadguru* works upon the human society intensely in a way so as to ensure that human beings transcend their human limitations and attain a limitless state of God, which is their original state.

Is it true that our Sadguru Shri Sai Baba used to take the sufferings of others?

The Sadgurus are without the bindings of any past Karma. In them, the seeds of all past *Karmas* both good and evil are burnt. They are in a state of *Karmik* 'vacuum'. As per the law of nature nothing can remain in a state of vacuum with any pressure from outside to fill up that vacuum. Therefore, the effects of *Karmas* of all living beings coming into their contact enter into that vacuum. This is the truth whether one knows it or not. This work is carried out by the *Sadgurus,* for all the souls coming into their contact in any manner what so ever. Whether the recipient of the Sadguru kindness wants it or not, is also not material because the 'law of compassion' of nature working through the *Sadguru* works spontaneously. For example, when a horse was beaten up at Shirdi, Baba's back bore the whip marks. This was a spontaneous reaction. Even the diseases and pains of the devotees are automatically transferred to the Guru. Whenever any devotee of Baba was in pain, Baba naturally used to experience it in His subtle body and some times in His physical body. The moment a devotee had a thought or *bhava* in his heart for Baba or called Him mentally, a vibration or a ray of subtle thought form instantly reaches the *Sadguru*. These secrets of nature are known by the Saints, yogis and evolved spiritual personalities. As Baba used to say "Be wherever you are and do whatever you like, I will know it even if I am thousands of miles away from you".

Because the past was imperfect and the future uncertain should we spoil the perfect present? While thinking of the imperfect past and uncertain future, we must not spoil the perfect present. In this world there has been on one whose past did not have imperfections or whose future is not uncertain.

Masters Disciples

How does one take time out to practice the "Guru Path" when one is under the constraint of time in our ordinary life?

Living even an ordinary life has been a difficult task with human beings in every age and not in the present time only. Leading an ordinary life means always trying to satisfy the social and family demands. It is easy for those who have left home and taken to ascetic way of life, to follow the spiritual path but it is a greater problem when living in our physical world looking after the never ending series of family and social commitments. We seek a Guru to give us a simple solution to this most difficult problem. In the first stage nobody follows the 'Guru Path' completely. It requires a number of years or attempts to prepare oneself. If a man goes on searching a Guru, reading books on this subject, reading the life stories of Saints, keeping purity in conduct etc., gradually the thoughts relating to the *Sadguru* will grow in his inner self. Under these conditions he will meet a Guru somewhere at a certain point of time. More correctly he will draw the attention of the Sadguru who has the divine power to see through the merits and demerits of everyone and the thought process of all His devotees even from a distance. It is said that the disciple cannot find a Guru, but the Perfect Master finds out His disciple certainly. As Baba said, "I draw my devotees from thousands of miles". In life full of difficulties it is a true endeavor to develop the qualities of compassion, forgiveness and service. Selfless service to all living beings is the goal of the Guru. It may be concluded that initially one should begin with obeying on smaller duties given to him by the Guru, and gradually one should move ahead for bigger jobs. While undergoing life's struggle whatever qualities one develops those remain permanently with him and become a part of his divine self. These qualities are carried to the next life. In the next life also he again gets the help of a Guru and evolves further. The Guru Path or Parampara is not a game of one life but of a time continuum.

What qualities a person needs to develop to evolve as a disciple and how?

The divine quality of a Guru or a disciple exists inherently in every human being. During childhood, parents impart children with elementary education necessary for their early growth. As they grow up they go to the schools and colleges and take formal education. In the normal course of life also one learns many things from different people and situations, knowingly or unknowingly. As far as it relates to the discipleship of a spiritual or religious Guru certain rules have to be followed. The first necessary quality to be a disciple is to have complete faith in the Guru that whatever the Guru is doing in relation to the disciple is in his best interest. The second is to try to follow the advice and instructions of the Guru to the best of one's abilities. For example, if the Guru says, "be kind and feed the poor", then one should do so as much as he is capable of doing. If problems arise during carrying-out of such instructions of the Master, then it should be tolerated and conveyed to Him. The true Guru will always give a solution to the problems faced by a disciple under every circumstance. The Guru will show the path that is suitable and easy for a devotee to follow in the complex and difficult world. Where the Guru is not in a physical form, there it would be proper to go through His preachings and find out the answer. That is why frequent reading of Shri Sai Satcharitra is always prescribed by me to all the devotees of Baba.

At the present time we hear about so many Gurus. How does one know if one has come across the true Guru or a Sadguru?

In the history of human civilization, every human being, at some point or the other, had the need of a Guru or a spiritual leader and he searched for him. It may be for educational, religious or spiritual or for any other purpose. All of us come across a number of teachers or Gurus in our life. It is said in "Guru Gita" that as a bee flees from a flower to a flower in search of honey, so the spiritual aspirant can also go from one Guru to another. Nothing wrong about it in the spiritual path so long as he is seeking a Sadguru. However, once he has found the Sadguru, then he should finally settle down and follow Him with single mindedness. All Gurus are not necessarily 'Sadgurus'. *Sadgurus* are those who are able to take the '*Atma*' of the devotee to '*Parmatma*', and who have the capability to protect the devotees under all circumstances and who can spiritually evolve the soul of the devotees and lead them towards the path of emancipation. Because of such capabilities they are known as 'Samarth' Gurus. There are very few Sadgurus who are *Jeevan Muktas* on this earth. Once a devotee establishes a spiritual relationship with the Sadguru then there is no further need to search for another Guru. One who wishes to progress spiritually in life must search for a Sadguru. Someday he will be able to draw the attention of the Sadguru if he continues to pray. Once the Master wants to draw him, then through some medium or the other He will pull him. The Master alone draws the disciple to Him by His own inscrutable ways at the right time. It is rarely that a disciple finds a real Master. Shirdi Sai used to pull His devotees from a distance as He is doing even now.

While treading the Guru path we are bound to commit mistakes. Should we convey them to the Guru?

Human beings are bound to commit mistakes. The *Sadguru* knows that his disciples will commit mistakes due to their ignorance known as '*maya*'. *Sadguru* always remains alert to stop the devotees from getting into the entrapments of maya. Because of his own mistake if a disciple falls into the danger then the '*Sadguru*' directly or indirectly helps him out. Baba used to say "Know it that wherever you are and whatever you do I am fully aware of it". Sai Baba's life history shows that He was omniscient, omnipotent and omnipresent. Guru alone knows how to take His disciples ahead spiritually and to stop him from committing mistakes. We certainly get protection of the Guru for the mistakes unknowingly done by us, but we should try to ensure that the mistakes knowingly committed are not repeated once they are pointed out to us. Sometimes we are not able to follow the path shown by the Guru due to circumstances and the Guru understands this since He is beyond the normal human qualities of anger and hatred. In His heart He has only compassion for His disciples. He keeps a watch on the intentions and motivations of the disciple for his spiritual evolution. If the devotee's will power is strong and there is complete surrender to the Guru then He goes on helping the disciple to evolve inspite of several mistakes committed by him.

There is unbound love between parent and child. Therefore children take complete liberty with the parents at times. Can a disciple also take that kind of liberty with his *Guru?*
There are various stages of relationship between the *Sadguru* and disciples. Such relationship grows slowly but surely as one travels along the path of spiritualism taking the Guru as the Guide or the father. One need not try always to know about this level of relationship frequently as it may create happiness or unhappiness, and may make a man egoistic because of his special relationship with his Guru. The internal guidance and support that the Master gives cannot be known easily by the disciple. Love is a spontaneous feeling of heart and therefore the liberty that a devotee takes with His Master has to be spontaneous. Before taking the liberties with the *Sadguru* as His child one has to work like His child- that is to take the responsibilities of his father and imbibe the qualities of the father. Is he prepared? It is not the "childish" but "child-like" quality that is appreciated by the Master. Baba had once asked a pertinent question to His devotees at Shirdi "How many devotees can be as good devotees to Baba as Baba was to His Guru." The child or the Ankita Santana of the Master has to have the divine qualities of the Master.

Shri Sai Satcharitra is full of examples of some of the children (Ankita Santana) of Baba taking liberties with Him. Tatya Kote Patil used to show his anger towards Baba and Shama used to use language which even friends would not ordinarily dare to utter before other friends. Baba also used to joke with them and tolerated all their impertinence because of their mutual bondage of love was pure and strong. Shri Sai Satcharitra is full of jokes that Baba used to cut with His devotees.

Then what should one do to become a perfect disciple?
To become the perfect disciple one has to follow the ideals of the Guru complete, achieve His powers and be a Guru himself at a point of time. But this is the highest achievement any disciple can think of

in his spiritual evolution. *Sadgurus* do not try to create disciples. They always try to evolve the soul of the disciple to their own level i.e. He wants to create more Gurus to help the mankind. This state is very high, and man himself becomes a perfect disciple when he imbibes the qualities of a Guru. But, before this stage is reached without loosing our patience, without setting the spiritual time-limit ourselves, without carving out a path for ourselves, as it normally happens in the world, we should be completely surrendered to the Guru and follow His path. First of all, we should be within His divine aura, then come near Him, then develop close bonds with Him, and try to complete all duties assigned by Him. With a bond of pure love with *Sadguru* one is bound to evolve spiritually. The Perfect disciple is the perfect reflection of a Perfect Master.

Many people say that Heaven lies at the feet of Guru. When and how one can experience this?

Washing and worshipping and serving the feet of a Sadguru is one out of the nine methods of devotion prescribed in Hinduism. After the Guru takes '*Samadhi*' i.e. leaves His physical body, one should meditate on His feet. Not only the feet but one should also meditate, according to Baba, from feet to head and from head to feet. To keep the feet of Guru in one's heart reflects the attitude of egolessness and serving Him and surrender. Here we do not bear the attitude of companionship (Sakha) with the Master but rather the attitude of being at His servant (Dasa). The worship of His feet means surrender at His feet and obeying His every command without questioning. A Sadguru is a reservoir of spiritual energy which flows through His feet. We are bound to receive that spiritual energy when we touch His feet.

I have been told that it is essential to have a living master to evolve spiritually. How true is it?

To have a living master is good. My personal experience is, if one prays to Baba even without a physical Master, one can evolve. I do not have any physical Master nor did I ever try. Baba is the *Param Sadguru* of this age. Baba said that He would be alive and helping His devotees from His tomb. I have been experiencing it to be true.

His body might have been entombed but His spirit is very much alive and continues to help His devotees. Ultimately everything depends on ones level of consciousness. At the initial stage a person entering the spiritual path needs to have a living Guru to guide him in the correct path.

The devotees desire to be with you always. When they are away from you they feel deprived. What is your reaction to this?

One who has taken Baba in his heart will never feel deprived or depressed. It is not necessary that a devotee should always stay near his Guru. The devotees who are very close to the Guru may be physically away from Him and those who are physically near Him may not be very close. The important thing is that what is the mental state (or Bhava) of a devotee towards his Spiritual Master? In my inner most thoughts there is no one else but Baba. Those who are close to Baba, I am close to them. I go along the *bhava* or the mental attitude of people. The temporal status or the external appearance of anyone is meaningless to me. The only important thing is that how single pointedly the devotee is looking towards Baba, and what is the level of his thinking and feelings? Besides this, nothing else has importance to me. This is what Baba has said a number of times.

Many people come to you for solution to their problems. Knowing the fact that their problems are an outcome of their own 'karmas', you pray to God for helping them. What is your reaction to this?

I can only pray to Baba to solve the problems of His devotees. My only appeal to *Sadguru* is that if He bestows His grace upon the distressed devotees then their sufferings would go away. Rest is on *Sadguru* or God. He will do as He may like to do. When anybody remembers God with a pure heart, and Shraddha (faith) he gets away from the shadows of bad effects. My effort is that the devotee should be inspired towards the right path to surrender to the Master.

> *The shortest distance between two points is a straight line.*
> *Therefore always adhere to the straight path in life.*

Faith and Devotion

At times our faith in Baba gets shaken up with the blow of a wind. How do we stop it and do not let it happen to us?

For these who want to come closer to Baba the only way is to keep unshakable faith in Him under all circumstances good, bad or neutral. But some people come to the Sadguru only with the desire of worldly gains or exhibit their devotion with such expectations hidden in their hearts. Sometimes, when their desires are not fulfilled or when they have to suffer the consequences of their own Prarabdha (past actions), they start blaming the Master and tend to lose faith. During the period of any *Avtaar* or *Sadguru* every wish of every man has never been fulfilled. *Sadguru*, never fulfills those desires, which would become barrier in the spiritual progress of the devotees. His hand can be seen behind both, the fulfillment and non fulfillment of the desires of the devotees. Therefore, one who can experience Baba both, in pleasure and pain, is the true devotee. The pleasure seekers are bound to deviate from the path as they don't seek the love of the Master but the material benefits; they wish to get from Him.

I have been going through a very trying time. Many times I feel that my faith is being tested, as Baba doesn't answer my prayers. How come I get no help from Baba?

Many actions are played by Baba from behind the scene for the benefit of the devotees which may not be known to the devotee themselves. Knowing the past 'Karmas' of a devotee, the Sadguru quietly works on his evolution. One has to have faith and patience to reap the benefits of His blessings in due course, and at a time ordained by Him. That is why Baba qualified the word *"Shraddha"* (faith) with the word *"Saburi"* (patience). Anyone of these two qualities cannot

Baba's Original Samadhi - Shirdi

Khandoba Temple – during Baba's Time

"Gurusthan" – During Baba's Time

Baba not visible in the photograph taken
without His permission

Baba surrounded by devotees at Dwarkamayee

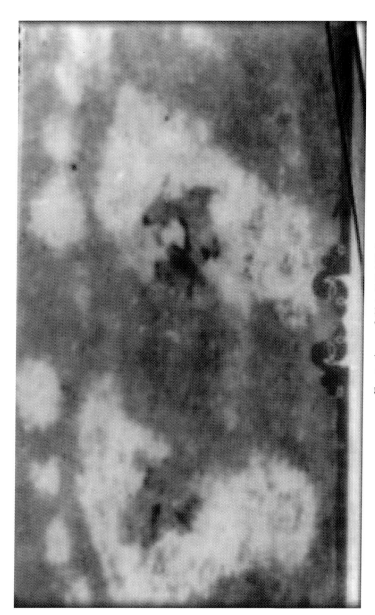

Footprints of Shirdi Sai Baba

stand without the other as they are inter-dependent. If you read "Shri Sai Satcharitra" you will get your answers as Baba did answer such queries of devotees in His own way.

The faith in Baba should never diminish. Will I be successful in achieving the same?

Read, think, speak, hear, write, meditate on Him as much as you possibly can. Use your entire faculties to understand Him. Try continuously and the candle of devotion will never be extinguished. It will go on shining brighter day by day.

Even though I am sincerely praying to Lord Baba and have a lot of faith in Him, I really don't think my problems are solved.

'Faith' with 'Patience' are the two key words that Baba prescribed for His devotees. Baba is always looking after His devotees in more than one ways, some of which the devotees do not know. Thousands of people are experiencing the help rendered by Baba today as they used to experience when Baba was at Shirdi in His human embodiment. Continue to pray. Life is a continuous process of problems and solutions. God does not solve it directly. He gets it done through us - that is through our *Karma* or actions, under the benevolent supervision of a Master or Sadguru. Sadgurus tell which Karmas (activities) are good and which are evil. He also knows when a problem is to be solved for the best benefit of the devotee. Please always have patience when leaving things at the hands of Baba to decide

I am an ardent devotee of Shri Sai Baba. I am facing lots of problems at present. Sometimes my faith in God starts dwindling and I feel there is nothing greater than destiny. Is my feeling correct?

I am sure that what you think to be a problem is not a problem but is certain type of an experience given to you by nature in order to evolve you. Destiny is always created by God, through a combination of circumstances and our own efforts. As per the Karma Theory of the Hindus nothing happens in life i.e. good or bad or neutral unless one has caused it to happen it through his actions in the past lives or in this life. In 'Shri Sai Sat Sachritra', Baba has advised His devotees not to be shaken by any problem whatsoever but to maintain patience and see what is coming in future while praying Him all the time. A wise devotee will always try to evolve or rebuild his destiny through the help of the Master. The Master can charter the course of His disciple much better in case the devotee has full faith in the Master (Shraddha) and lots of patience (Saburi).

I believe in Shirdi Sai Baba and have His picture and idol in my house. Recently, a thief came to my house and stole some money and things. My faith was a bit shaken because I thought that Baba will protect my house from such untoward events. Should I dismiss events like this as Baba's wish?

Please read Shri Sai Satcharitra. It will give you lots of answers through examples. If one loses faith by entry of an intruder in his house, then one should lose faith in himself when a bad thought enters his mind leading to evil activities. Bad thoughts are like a thieves who steals away our good quality and virtues. The true devotees will see the *Sadguru* in both good and bad and pleasurable and harmful aspects of life. Please try strengthening your faith and have patience if you want to progress. Even when a Sadguru is there to help, human tendencies like greed, anger, jealously of other human beings around Him does not come to a sudden halt. Due to the influence of the Master the evil qualities slowly reduce.

We want to be good and give pure love to Baba but, we do not know how? Please help us in this regard. When and how a human being becomes a good devotee?

Love cannot be organized and practiced the way most of the people think. It is a spontaneous feeling and process of a heart. To love Baba means one has to accept Him as the main or even sole objective of life. One has to concentrate ones thought, time and energy to come closer to the Master. While loving the Master (i.e. Shraddha), one must also have a lot of patience (i.e. Saburi). The real test of faith is in patience under adverse circumstances.

If one is able to awaken the divine qualities like compassion, forgiveness, human service, non-violence, etc. within oneself then the Sadguru helps him and walks along with him. It is evident from reading Shri Sai Satcharitra that those who had completely surrendered to Baba were close to Him e.g. Kaka Saheb Dixit, Megha, Mhalsapati and others. External worship and rituals are only methods of inner self purification. However, any amount of worship does not qualify a Sai devotee to be close to Shri Sai if his inner thought process is not clean.

I am a new and simple devotee of Baba, but sometimes I am unable to pray to Baba with concentration. How do I get more devotion towards Baba?

Baba had asked His devotees to remember Him not only in the biggest but also in the smallest activities and objects around us. Remember Him before entering sleep, after waking from sleep, before taking food, before using any new item, before starting any new profession etc. There is no limitation or restriction of time, place or situation for remembering Baba and associating our consciousness with Him in every mundane activity that we do besides the religious ones. This is one of the easiest ways of devotion. By doing so continuously one will develop concentration and establish an inner relationship with Him.

Pray to Him in any form suited to your emotions – a master, a father, a mother, a friend, etc. Loving God is the best prayer for God. Prayers generate love and if love is there, formal prayers are not necessary. Read Shri Sai Satcharitra, depicting the life history of Baba for further directions. Visit *Shirdi* early if you have not. There is a lot of material on Baba on the internet. You can go through them. If you do so, your evolution is surely going to take place though gradually. Hence be patient and steadfast which Baba termed as 'Saburi' when proceeding in the path of Shraddha (devotion).

How do we get pure love towards Baba?

It comes gradually through our efforts and by His grace. Faith with patience is required which Baba termed as *Shraddha - Saburi*. Love does not develop by sheer intellectual understanding of love. It grows like an organic body slowly and imperceptibly. One has to try consistently. Read, think, and speak of Baba's deeds and sayings. When Baba becomes a part of your consciousness, love will become intense.

Try to work for His cause as well, whenever you get a chance and help the poor, diseased and needy, wherever you can in the name of Baba.

Will Sai Baba ever give His *darshan* to me?

Usually the word Darshan means the physical Darshan through the cognitive faculty of the eyes. When Baba was at Shirdi people used to have His Darshan. There are also references that devotees like Mankar at Macchindragada, Mhalsapati at the bank of the river Godavari got Baba's Darshan. Further many people had Darshan of Baba in their dreams. In case your devotion is very intense and stable over a long period of time you have a chance of having His Darshan in dreams.

Physical *darshan* of a Sadguru is when He is in the physical body. Later, through deep meditation one can have his *darshan* internally. Pray to Shri Sai always to bless you with His *swaroop darshan*.

How do I get close to Baba? How do I feel His presence and get assured that He is with me?

You have to love Him. Keep Him as an image in your heart. Serve human beings and other living species as part of Him. The process is gradual; but continue to try. You have to see His presence in everything and in all. He is all the time with you, but you don't know. When you will fully understand this, you will surely feel His presence always. When the Master enters a devotee or captures his heart and mind, he starts feeling differently. He feels emotionally charged towards Him, and likes to read, hear and talk about Him always and when working for Him he works like a possessed person.

Sometimes I get tears when I think of Baba. I don't know the reason for that.

Baba sends love waves to His devotees all the time. When it touches the heart of the devotee he feels emotional towards Him. This happens with thousands of people. These are tears of strength not weakness. Keep loving Baba. He will grow in you.

I am very much drawn to Sai Baba, and I consider myself His devotee, but I have trouble keeping Him in mind throughout

the day. I would like Him to be constantly present in my mind and heart. Does this come by His grace only?

Your thought process is noble and correct. Don't worry at all if you can't keep Him in your mind constantly because you have to do other things also where mind has to be applied. Baba is aware of your problems. Please continue to connect the thought of Baba with whatever you do and as much as you can do i.e. good or bad or neutral. Slowly but surely you will feel that your mind is unconsciously getting aware about the Master, in whatever you might be doing. Do not worry if sometimes you can't capture Him in your mind. After some time it will happen automatically.

Many devotees give lot of importance to the miracles exhibited by Saints. What is your opinion regarding this?

Generally, the word miracle means a certain happening or phenomena about which ordinary human beings are ignorant. For example, removal of disease through a touch of hand or materialization of objects from air or giving accurate warning about coming events in a man's life by the Spiritual Masters are taken as miracles. Actually these are not miracles; but these take place because of the subtle divine powers used by the Spiritual Masters and other Saints about which we are ignorant. Since these Masters handle hundreds of souls at a given point of time together, they cannot do so like the ordinary human beings using their gross body or mind. Around Shri Shirdi Sai Baba such miracles used to happen in plenty and lots of devotees used to be benefited. The life of Shri Krishna and Lord Christ is also full of such miracles. When people get benefitted through the use of unknown and un-imaginable powers of the Masters, their devotion towards the Masters gets enhanced. Such Masters are called the "Samarth" Gurus. However, some devotees think that all their problems should be solved by the Masters through such miracles. Their desire for miracles sometimes overtakes their devotion and this is where the problem starts. Priority should be given to devotion (Bhakti) over miracles. A real devotee will never request the Guru to create miracles for the satisfaction of his material needs. He will only pray to the Sadguru for His mercy and to lead him in any manner that He (Master) likes.

**How to win Sai's love? Though I do everyday *Pooja*, Sai
Sacharitra *parayan* and His *naam smarana* still I don't feel
His presence like I did in the past. I want His assurance like
He used to give me before.**

One of the assurances given by Baba to his devotees is, "If you take
one step towards Me, I shall take ten steps towards you". Baba's love
never ends, dwindles or changes with the situations of the world or
the changes in the devotee. He is constantly there with you. He is the
only 'Constant' in your life whereas all other factors like job, family,
society are 'Variables'. Such a feeling shows that your faith is being
tested. Soon He will assure you in a certain manner provided you are
honest and steadfast in your prayer. Don't worry over temporary
disturbances, which are bound to arise from time to time.

**Why the *Sai* name does not echo in our mind constantly, and
what effort should we do to make it work?**

The chanting of a "name" going on continuously and spontaneously
in us even if we are not conscious of it is called '*ajapa jap*'. It goes on
continuously and effortlessly like our breathing cycle (i.e. inhalation
and exhalation). The best process of naam smarana is one when it
goes on spontaneously like our breath cycle. We do not make any
conscious efforts to repeat our breaths; it goes on in its own rhythm.
When we synchronize, the chanting of the name with our breath
cycle then the result of mantra chanting or naam samarana becomes
more effective. A householder may find it difficult to do so because
his mind in frequently diverted towards various worldly activities. It
is better that we try to remember the word '*Sai*' with every breath or
without chanting keep His thought in mind whenever possible.
Gradually, it will unconsciously become a continuous inner process
within us. Every work and thought should be linked with His
thoughts. This could be a type of *mental jaap* or *Manasa jaap* for the
householder.

---

*We have to be kind to others to receive kindness of the
Sadguru.*

Worship and Prayers

Please teach me how to do the prayers of Shirdi Sai Baba. What is the best method of praying?

Place Baba's statue or photograph in front of you. Begin by concentrating on His photograph or painting from feet to head and vice-versa as Baba has himself prescribed in chapter 22 of Shri Sai Satcharitra. Either sing the *Aarti* of Baba or recite any *Mantra* you know or pray through a familiar language. This is so because one must clearly understand the meaning of the Aarti or Bhajans that he is singing in the name of the Master. What is necessary is a feeling of love towards Him. Silent and concentrated prayer is the best. One can pray at any time and at any place silently. Mental prayer with concentration is better, in case the devotee has developed that capacity. Otherwise, pray aloud individually or in congregations as is generally practiced at home or in the temples.

I very much want to get closer to Baba, both through prayers and meditation. Although, things go smoothly, I often feel that all the progress that I have made is lost when I am afflicted by Maya. What is the way to be more steadfast in one's principles?

Living amidst the worldly conditions termed as *Maya,* one cannot avoid this situation unless one decides to leave the worldly activities totally and become a *yogi* or a *Sanyasi.* He will be less afflicted by maya, if one holds on to Baba always in some form say, taking His name, speaking about Him to others, reading about Him, thinking about Him etc, the mind gets His support to sustain and develop the inner power to resist the attacks of *Maya.* More strong the attraction towards Baba develops less strong will be the attraction towards the illusory worldly aspects.

I want to perform Pooja two to three times a day for Baba, which I used to do. Though at the back of mind He is always there I want to do much more. I am a working married woman. How do I manage my time for Baba's worship?

Do not worry if you cannot do formal *pooja* as others do under more convenient circumstances. *If* a small *pooja* before going out and before sleep is done it is fine. You can even do mental *pooja* through concentration wherever you are. Constant and loving remembrance of Baba in whatever manner is the best path and the best pooja. Read Shri Sai Satcharitra daily and you will find the answers.

Does my prayers and feelings reach Baba and my Guru? Sometimes I feel like having a feedback on this. How do I know their response?

The moment a prayer is spoken or is made silently by a devotee his thought reaches Baba instantaneously. Baba had assured that "Wherever you are, whatever you do, always remember this one thing well, that all that you do is known to Me." Therefore continue to remember Him and pray patiently. In due course of time you will surely get what you call "feedback" or "indication" in some manner some day from the Guru. Thousands of devotees of Baba experience Baba's grace in this manner and are convinced of Baba's acceptance of their prayers and feelings.

What is the meaning of "OM SAI, SRI SAI, JAYA JAYA SAI"?

This is a mantra formulated for Shri Sai Baba of Shirdi and is universally accepted by all His devotees. The word "Om" placed at the beginning of the mantra is an additional attachment to the original mantra. In most of the Hindu mantras "Om", "Aum" or "Pranav tattwa" the primordial energy form of the creation of the universe is placed before the mantra itself. Jaya Sai means "Glory to Sai" or "Hail Sai" and Shri Sai is invocation of Shri Sai.

What is the correct way to meditate on Baba's form or repeat His name or merely remember Him silently if one does not have time to follow a prescribed spiritual procedure?

Just keep on remembering Him at the back of your mind while carrying on the routine duties of life. Whenever you have little time say 15 minutes or 10 minutes even take His name. When time permits, meditate on His form even when sitting on a chair. If all the three can be done together it is the best. Since God has created everything, He has to be seen and experienced in all aspects of the seen and unseen world in which we live. One has to undergo all the worldly experiences with the belief that these are necessary for the progress of the human soul as ordained by Nature or God or *Sadguru*. However, if one can have a fixed time, everyday to carry on certain religious or spiritual practices like meditation, it is the best. The inner thought process will slowly get stabilised in a short time.

What is *"Gayatri Mantra"?* When, how and where should one practice *"Gayatri Mantra"?*

Gayatri Mantra is the most potent mantra of Hinduism that should be remembered and chanted by every Hindu and for that matter by every human being. This is a universal *mantra* and is meditated and chanted not only for one's own good but also for the good of others. It is both a *mantra* and a prayer. Therefore, it can be practiced with ease and spontaneity. One should chant or meditate on this while facing the Sun. In the morning recite it facing the East, at noon facing the North and in the evening when facing the West. Unless specifically prescribed by a capable Guru, one should never recite it at midnight facing South. *During jaap* one can either externally or internally concentrate on the statue of Gayatri or on Sun or on the Guru. Gayatri is *Parashakti* (Primordial energy form of the universe) from whom the universes evolve. Recitation of Gayatri Mantra generates various types of powers including occult powers in the practitioner. It purifies the mind of the practitioner.

By what method Baba's worship should be done at home?

There is a basic difference between the worship of Baba done at home and in a temple. The *'Praan Pratishtha'* (installation of a statue) is not usually done for the idol at home; where generally His photograph or a small statue is worshipped. Therefore, any *'Panchopachar'* pooja method can be adopted to worship Baba at home where as in temple *'Shodopachar'* pooja is done. It is necessary to simplify the method of worship of the Sadguru. Most of the external rites and rituals are artificial if they do not evoke inner *bhakti*. Offering even a single flower with *bhava* and with unshakeable faith to the *Sadguru* is sufficient. If we are away from home for some reason, we can still worship Baba the same way as we do at home mentally, sitting in a place or while travelling in a train or vehicle. This is called 'Manas Puja'. At home the formal pooja can be assigned to anybody else. Baba is beyond any discrimination of religion, caste or creed, small or big, rich or poor.

It is said in the Vedas that the power of all the Hindu deities are inherent in the form of the *Sadguru*. So there is nothing wrong if only the Sadguru is worshipped at home or if He is worshipped in the form and manner of any deity. Sikh devotees sacrificed their lives happily for their Gurus because it was their belief that the Guru is eternal and will always be with them. It is absolutely necessary to have immense faith in the *Sadguru* and worship Him as God. Whereas Puja is a methodology, Bhakti is the substance of spiritualism.

I have got a small statue of Baba. In which direction Baba's idol or image should be installed?

Baba's statue or image can be placed facing any direction. In Dwarkamayi Masjid He was sitting facing east. In Gurusthan He was sitting facing west. In the Samadhi His head is towards North. However His statue in the Samadhi Mandir faces east. It is best that His statue faces east, north or north east.

Is it necessary to prepare something different to offer to Baba? Is there any particular food item required for offering to Baba?

Most of the devotees treat Baba not only as their God but also as the head of their family. Hence whatever is cooked at home for ourselves the same should be offered to Baba and can be distributed among others as *Prashad*. Whatever is offered to Him with a pure thought will be acceptable to Him. In certain forms of worship offering non-vegetarian food to the deity is prescribed. It is only our love or *"bhava"* behind such offerings, which is accepted by the Sadguru. The rich and poor alike can offer whatever is possible within their means. The quality or quantity of offerings is not material. What is important is the quality of thought through which it is offered.

When and how should an ordinary man worship Baba or meditate on Him?

We worship God to experience Him. The various methods of worship are different ways to reach Him but it is not the goal in itself. Our goal is Baba. Many people have realized God without following any conventional methods of worship. However for the beginners it would be best to meditate on Baba for some time in the morning or at night. Worship Him in a normal way but with intense devotion; always regard Him as a part of one's life. Whatever you eat offer Him and offer every activity and feelings – happy or sad, of yours to Him. If we always remember Him and pray Him it would be a form of uninterrupted worship. All the time bearing Baba in mind is the real worship - this is spontaneous worship. To love Baba is the best form of worship of Baba.

If one wants to conduct formal worship at home then morning time is the most suitable as the mind is in a peaceful condition and one is not disturbed by the worldly activities. Worship Baba in the morning in the traditional way with *Aarti,* offer flowers, *naivedya* etc. Before going to sleep also worship Him, put *Udhi* on forehead, take a pinch in the mouth, remember His name and go off to sleep. This is the traditional method of worship of Baba.

What should we ask Baba in our prayers?

Our first prayer to Baba should be to free us from the bad thoughts and actions i.e. *paap,* of body and mind and the debts (Rinanubandha) generated through our past lives. Before we ask for Baba's grace we should request Baba to make us worthy of His grace. It is necessary to become worthy of His grace before yearning to receive it. If we want the Master or God to shower His grace on us we should be graceful and kind to others including animals. Unless we have these qualities we can't appreciate them in others. Kindness towards others is sure to beget kindness of Baba towards us.

Please teach me the best method to do the prayers of Shirdi Sai Baba.

Begin by concentrating on His photograph from feet to head and vice-versa as Baba has himself prescribed in Shri Sai Satcharitra. Either pray through a familiar language or singing the *Aarti* of Baba or recite any *Guru Mantra* you know. What is necessary is generating a feeling of love towards Him. Every silent but truthful prayer is acceptable to the Master. One can pray at any time and at any place silently. Mental prayer with concentration is better than external prayer in case the devotee has developed that capacity. Otherwise do Aarti or pray aloud alone or with others as is generally practiced at home, temples or other devotional congregations.

I want to be close to Baba. I worship Him not with prayers, incense sticks etc. but I only sing some *bhajans* twice a week. I do not hurt others. Can I improve myself further?

Living in the worldly life which is full of stress and strain, one must find some time to remember the Master in any way i.e. by reading, singing, thinking or speaking about Baba. One can do pooja at home as well. One can render devotion to God or Master in any one or more methods of devotion. In any case singing the glory of Baba is one of the *"Navadha Bhaktis"* (i.e. *nine methods of expression of devotion).* Not hurting others is a good state of mind but positively helping others to the extent possible without expecting rewards or fame is a better act. Helping others even when one gets hurt from them is a far more superior condition of mind. It is a divine attribute.

When Sai Himself is one with Lord Ganesha, why should we pray Lord Ganesha at the beginning of Sai pooja. In Sai temples, even Sri Lakshmi Astotram is being chanted in Sai pooja. I understand that Baba is Sri Vishnu and I assume, therefore Sri Lakshmi pooja is done? I stopped doing Lakshmi pooja for about 4 years, and now I restarted the same assuming the above reason. Please enlighten me.

In Shirdi, during Baba's time, some devotees used to worship other deities like Ganesha, Shiva, Pandharinath etc., while simultaneously worshipping Baba. Baba never objected to it. There were a few devotees who used to worship Baba only and not any other deity. Some others used to worship Baba in the form, mantra and method of the worship of other deities like Shri Ganesha, Shiva, Hanumaan, etc. Hindu scriptures hold that a Sadguru can be worshipped in the form of any deity. The Sadguru is a complete Spiritual Entity in Himself. Therefore the mantra reads, 'Gurur Brahma, Gurur Vishnoo, Guru deva Maheshwara'. Hence if the Sadguru is worshipped alone, it is alright.

How do I focus on the physical form of Baba when I know that He is not living in His physical body now?

Initially focus on the physical form of Baba as you see Him in his statues, photos and paintings etc. Gradually you will be able to perceive Him in a subtle form. Please continue to meditate on Him consistently, then He may reveal His real self to you. This method of meditation is mentioned in Shri Sai Satcharitra.

Many people speak of Manasa Pooja. What is Manasa Pooja and how to do it?

Manasa Pooja means going through the entire process of Pooja that we usually do sitting in front of a statue or a picture (in our case it is Shri Sai Nath Maharaj), through a mental process. For example, when we are doing a normal pooja we are looking at the statue, offering Naivedya, holding a lamp and doing Aarti also. While doing so, we are looking at all these things and all around the place as well and completing the entire process of pooja stage by stage. In Manasa Pooja also, such pooja activities are done by mentally picturising the same process and same stages within the same time scale. The eyes remain closed and the devotee focuses his inner-mind on the statue / picture in front. He goes on performing each stage of pooja like bathing, clothing, decorating the statue, offering Naivedya, and doing Aarti in front of the mental image of Baba, as if it was real. While doing so the worshipper does not cut-short on the time of the actual pooja. Initially it is difficult to do Manasa Pooja, but after lots of practice Manasa Pooja becomes easy. The benefit of such a pooja system is that it can be done at any place and at any time. However, it is advisable to do pooja at the usual pooja time of the day even when one is away from home.

I have been a follower of Sai Baba and I have always believed that I am doing the right thing by praying to Baba & seeking His blessings instead of the support of a Guru, Lately, I have started reading some literature which emphasizes on the importance of having a Guru to support and guide. I am thoroughly confused. I staunchly believe that I can pray to Baba directly and seek whatever I am looking for directly from Him.

Our soul reflected as our conscience is our inner Guru. The Guru and Saints influence that inner self and through it evolve the devotee. What you are doing is fine. Read books on Baba, think about Him and have *Satsang* i.e. exchanging experience with other devotees. When a Sadguru like Baba is in your heart a physical Guru may not be necessary. Take Baba as a physically existing Guru. However, at times the Sadgurus, send an intermediary worker or spiritual guide to help the devotee. If such an intermediary guide is available one should take his help.

Do not ponder over negative traits in others, for then they will take root in you. On the other hand if you ponder on the good traits in others, those will grow in you.

WORSHIP AND PRAYERS

Devotees offering prayers to Baba

GOD, RELIGION, PATH AND PHILOSOPHY

Baba Surrounded by devotees from different religious sects

God, Religion, Path and Philosophy

Everyone speaks of God. I want to know who is God or what is God?

This is a question which the entire human civilization on this earth has been trying to understand since the time immemorial, yet nobody can exactly say who is God. Even the greatest spiritual leaders in the world, the Vedas and other religious scriptures have admitted their limitations in fully comprehending these concepts regarding God beyond a certain point. The Seers try to experience and understand God from His manifested aspects - both living (Sakara) and non-living (Nirakara) and seen and unseen. After realising the manifested aspects of God like the stars, planets, living and non-living beings, the Saints enter into the non-manifested (Nirakara) aspects of God to a certain extent. It is said that God has manifested only one-fourth of His energy and that three-fourth of God's energy lies within Him and is not manifested. How then to understand the non-manifested three-fourth aspect in the God when the entire humanity has not been able to understand even the one-fourth manifestation? That is why it is easier to understand the Sadguru as the form of God rather than try to understand God Himself.

How to understand the unlimited God when our human intelligence is so limited?

Every soul in the process of its evolution, life after life, is trying to understand and experience God within himself and in the outside world. In fact, this progressive understanding of God through a series of lives is the real purpose of human birth. Human beings are better equipped with cerebral capacity than a monkey or ape (from which stage he evolves). It is for understanding God at the first stage and then realizing God at the ultimate stage that the human being has been endowed with these capabilities of nature. Man is superior to all other animals not only because he has more evolved physical and mental machinery but because he has the capacity to imagine, accept, seek and realize God. All religions and scriptures have prescribed the methods to realize God. These are known as the different paths. All the realized souls and saints have also spoken about the same. Baba used to tell His devotees at Shirdi that many paths lead to God. One of the paths goes through Shirdi, meaning thereby the path shown by Him. Any devotee following the path shown by Shri Sai Nath Maharaj will someday realize God. If we surrender to the Master we will be able to understand God through His intelligence.

We are told that God is there in the living and the non living. Is there any *Dharma* for the non-living aspects of God beyond the living aspects of God?

Dharma in the real sense of the term means the existence of a whole by holding together the parts. It is not only the formal *Dharmas* like Hinduism or Christianity. *Dharma* is all pervasive in the universe. It covers both the living and non-living aspects of universe. When the different life forms had not evolved on this earth, it was an earth consisting of material forces like water, earth, fire, air and a sky. It is through the process of evolution of nature that the non-living forces created the living form and forces. Therefore even after the living, including human beings were created; the seen and unseen interaction between the living and the non-living continues. These two elements of living and non-living are so much interdependent that if the relation between the living and the non-living forces are not balanced then chaos will be created on earth. Think of a simple example i.e. if all the coal or oil of the earth is over spent or wasted by human beings without planning then how can we get energy and power once they get exhausted. That is where necessity to use the supports of nature in a balanced manner is so essential. In the sky, we see the Stars, including our Sun and Planets, moving in a certain order in accordance with their *Dharma*. Any little deviation in their path can create havoc. Can you imagine that!

Today the whole world is experiencing and trying to look at this problem of inter-relationship between the living and the non living in a different way which is called 'ecological balance' or protection of the environment. When this balance is not achieved between the human beings and the non-living things, great problems takes place e.g. if we contaminate air or water then diseases are bound to affect us. *Dharma* is therefore, not only a spiritual and religious side of things, it also means a way of living together whether in a family, society, country or world. Here the self-limitation of the individuals or the scriptural limitations imposed on individuals for the greater good of the good of the other living species is a matter of paramount importance. Therefore, *Dharma* can be defined as the best way of living together with all the forces of nature, both (living and non-living) under all circumstances for the longest period of time on this earth and in this universe.

We are not Saints or Sadgurus like Baba. Since we are ordinary people, how can we understand the existence and form of God?

God is present in innumerable energy forms both seen and unseen in this Universe. He is present in every particle in the universe in gross, subtle and energy forms. His visible manifested form is the visible and non-visible Universe. On the basis of the principle of *Vyasthi* (individual) and *Samashti* (group), whatever is there in every part of the Nature is also there in the Whole, and whatever is there in the Whole is also present in its part. In every star there is an energy form called 'Vishnu' and in Sun there is an energy form called 'Narayan'. Therefore we worship and propitiate the sun by calling it as 'Surya Narayan'. In every universe the basic creative energy flows from two specific terminals. One is continuously creating the building materials of the universe and the other is sending the vital force (Prana) which holds the material universe together. When we say - Vishnu and Mahavishnu, Deva and Mahadeva, Ganapati and Mahaganpati, Shiva and Sadashiva- – they are symbolic representation of the different energy forms only. In fact, the form of God can be experienced through limited as well as unlimited manifestations and concepts. God exists because we exist and we exist because God exists. If we are not conscious then can we think of God or consciousness. Therefore we can understand God through our consciousness only.

Why do we symbolize God through human forms?

Because it is impossible to comprehend the cosmic form of God (both micro and macro), through concepts and imaginations of the human race. Because the brain capacity of the human beings is limited it can't hold the unlimited. Therefore, through the use of symbols like statues and paintings we can have the personal experience of His form and attributes. God has been incarnating in different forms including human forms to make His identity easier for us to experience. Otherwise it is impossible to behold the form of God consisting of millions of stars and galaxies.

Can human intellect comprehend God?

God is not any single or limited concept, which can be defined with our limited intellect or knowledge. He is the synthesis of millions of such concepts of nature from atoms to universe that emanated from Him only. The intellectual knowledge of the human beings is based on concepts, and such concepts emanate from our limited knowledge. A large number of Saints and Sadgurus never had any formal education. They never had the intellectual achievements like being professors, scientists, bureaucrats or writers. Nevertheless divine concepts came to them spontaneously because they followed the path of Bhakti and practised simplicity in their lives. Through yoga practices some of them increased the utilisation capacity of their brain and then only could they visualise the micro and macro capacities of God.

If there is one God, then why are there so many religions on this earth? Should a person change his religion?

It is only God, the Almighty or the Divine force that is responsible to create the human beings, sustain them and also to bring about their physical end which we term as death. All this is true for the living human beings. All these beings carrying human souls are scattered all-over this earth. They are born in different social, cultural and geographic situations. Each one has a certain level of consciousness, and a series of experience carried through a few lives. The experiences and levels of consciousness of each of them may be similar, but cannot be the same. God creates different religions for the evolution of different groups of souls who are required to follow a certain path which a religion prescribes. In fact, religions have been created differently through different Incarnations to evolve different groups of souls at different places and at different points of time. Any person who is born in one religion should therefore, stick to it because without experience of the path prescribed by that religion, he cannot further evolve. So Geeta clearly tells us *"Swadharme nidhana shreyah, Parodharma Vayavaha"* which means it is better to die for one's own religion, than accept any other religion.

If religions are different, do the various Incarnations bring about these differences?

Religions are different as they prescribe different methods to seek God even though they ultimately strive to lead all human beings to the same goal - God realisation. However, the Incarnations like Buddha, Christ or Prophets are nothing but the human manifestations of the same God at different places and at different points of time. Here the 'will' to create different religions is that of God and He incarnates in different forms. Therefore, the human embodiment's purpose and method may be different but Incarnations in the ultimate analysis are the same. They create a certain religion which in other words is a certain way of life for groups of souls for whom that path of religion is necessary for their evolution.

If all religions have emanated from God, then why do people fight on religions issues?

If all human beings were that perfect in their understanding of life, then there was no need for God to incarnate and establish so many religions. Only because human beings with their limitations of their mind have a natural tendency to differ and antagonize each other, therefore, religions and spiritual teachers like the Sadgurus try to show them different ways at different points of time to get out of their self created problems and limitations. The main problem is that after the departure of the incarnations, interpretations of His sayings or preachings are carried out by some of the religions leaders, who are imperfect and at times don't understand the lofty principles of the

Masters. Some of them, even while displaying religious sentiments, interpret the original sayings of the incarnations in a way which is in contradiction to what the incarnation Himself had propounded. Common people, not knowing the difference between the intentions of the real incarnations and the interpretation prescribed by these leaders follow them blindly. This leads to fanaticism, rivalry and even wars. Whenever situation deteriorates beyond a point and people suffer due to wrong, narrow or bigoted interpretation of religion or way of life, God again incarnates and reestablishes *Dharma*. This has been going on since time immemorial and will also continue in future.

Religions are different, but is there anything common in them, I mean are there any common parameters?

All religions believe in the existence of a Supreme Being called God. The word *Dharma* comes from the Sanskrit (root word Dhru) which means to hold together. Religions, therefore try to hold together not only different human beings or groups of people, but also the other creations of nature like plants, animals, birds etc. As ordained by nature they live together and are inter-dependent. Therefore they must be held in a fine balance of mutual existence. The principles for holding them together for the greatest good of the greatest number for the longest period of time are known as *Dharma*. The concepts of Hindu universalism, the Muslim brotherhood, the missionary spirit of service of the Christians and the Buddhist concept of tolerance are nothing but different methods to establish and enforce the common denominators of togetherness. Human beings are aware of these principles but lose their path from time to time. Then incarnations advent in human embodiment to re-establish these concepts of love, tolerance, sacrifice, unity and simplicity which holds them together.

Could you please tell me if Sai Baba has commented in any way on the Hare Krishna movement and on Chaitanya Mahaprabhu?

Shri Chaitanya was an incarnation of love. There is no difference between Hari (means one who takes away sorrows) and Krishna, the Incarnation of God. Baba encouraged everyone to follow his own religion and path, but always emphasized on selfless love, faith and patience. Baba had very high regards for Lord Krishna as Krishna Janmashtami used to be celebrated at Shirdi regularly.

I just learned about Sai Baba today. Is He the reincarnation of Jesus on earth?

Shri Shirdi Sai is an incarnation of the 19th century A.D. His role on earth has been like that of Jesus, - kindness personified, the most merciful man to redeem humanity of its misery. No incarnation re-incarnates. Only God comes to the earth with different incarnations.

I would like to know what the relationship between Baba and Jesus is. And if I believe in Jesus, can I believe in Baba too?

All incarnations are manifestation of God. The Almighty works differently at different points of times and in different societies and at different places. There is a lot common between Baba and Christ i.e. love, self -sacrifice, living like ordinary persons among their disciples etc. Even I believe in Jesus as the kindest redeemer of millions of human beings.

If God is one, why should there be different paths?

God manifests Himself in different forms. Even as a human form He manifests Himself at different places, at different times with different levels of consciousness. Groups of souls having different levels of consciousness are born in different places and times and groups of souls having the same experience are at times born at the same place or as a same grouping. These groups of souls are so born because they are required to experience certain common religious, social, geographic etc. situations necessary for their evolution. For example, a group of souls may be born from parents belonging to one religion or belonging to a certain country. In the next life, to have different experience, some of these souls may be born of parents having a different religions or belonging to different countries or nationalities. Many Hindus became Buddhists when Lord Buddha incarnated and many Hindus came back to Hinduism later at the time of Adi Shankaracharya. Therefore, there are different ways of evolution of the souls. Ultimately, all these paths converge at one point i.e. God realisation or in God from where they all emanated.

Why do some people change their religion or path in one life?

A human soul is generally born with the experience of same paths or religions, he had adopted in the earlier lives. However, in certain cases in the next life he is born of parents of a different religion from the one he had adopted in earlier life. The past lives' experiences, even if, he does not remember, do manifest as a part of his behaviour, thinking and conduct in the later life. Thus, some people go back to their earlier path due to such 'samskara' or if the jiva gets saturated with the experience of one path, they get into another path. While doing so people may think logically of having done a volitional act of having changed a religion or a path, but in the ultimate analysis, this thinking process itself is pre-ordained due to past Karmas, which generate clear cut propensities in human minds. Experiences of the earlier lives at times propel us to have the same experiences in this life also.

How can a human being make rapid progress in the direction of spiritual evolution?

Nobody can progress in the spiritual path by merely reading or listening to others or planning his spiritual development as a time-bound management concept. Any such knowledge, which is not put into practice, shall not be of much use. It is not easy to practice the code of conduct required in the spiritual path e.g. to be egoless and to sacrifice for others etc. For doing this, faith in the Master and God and will power are absolutely necessary. It becomes possible and easier for the devotee to tread this path by surrender at the feet of a *Sadguru* or a Master. A worldly man should not try to become a *Yogi*, a *Siddha*, or to awaken one's *Kundalini* or to become a liberated soul etc. It would be a foolish act to use these phrases for oneself without understanding their meaning. It is important to have unshakable faith in God and pray Baba continuously to lead us in the path as ordained by the laws of nature. We must also understand this fact that we are not the doers. It is necessary to do away with the sense of doership. This sense of being a doer emerges from our ego and does not leave us easily. Once we follow the path shown by the Sadguru or the Master with devotion and patience then if the *Sadguru* wants He may give us *siddhi* or *mukti* or whatever He desires but we should not strive for the same through our limited and sometimes distorted perceptions.

Why the mind is not under full control even if we try for it? Can one expedite the eligibility for His Grace to realize the happiness borne out of complete faith?

Peace of mind will only come by the grace of the Master, when one is eligible for it. Eligibility will come through a continuous process of uplifting one's virtues by speech, conduct and thought. This is possible if one surrenders to Him. Striving with faith and patience towards the path will bring the grace of the Sadguru.

While treading the path towards Baba if a devotee feels surrounded by despair, what should he do?

I have said in one of my poems – *"Jab dil udaas ho to Sai ka naam lena"* i.e. "When one feels depressed one should take the name of Sai". Human beings have a tendency to feel depressed at times, when facing the pain and miseries of life. But, if such feeling of pain and misery are true, so are the feelings of joy and bliss. One should see the role of Shri Sai in both the situations. In happiness without wasting too much time in rejoicing, if we can help others in getting the same happiness in Baba's name or work for the cause of Baba then the happiness that we derive will be more lasting. Physical happiness is momentary and once it is gone it brings sorrow as mind has a tendency to yearn for the same or more happiness always, which certainly is not possible in anybody's life. Whenever you are in sorrowful situation remember Baba's words. "Keep your balance and see what comes next". Keeping in touch with Baba internally and thinking of Him reduce sorrow. By reading Shri Sai Satcharitra, by singing Baba's *bhajans* the sorrow gets certainly lessened. In bad times one must read about Baba as much as one can, meditate on Him, chant His name, sing His devotional songs and help other people who are in greater distress than us.

When man knows that he is fallen, and therefore not qualified to tread the spiritual path then what should he do?

To this day there has not been any human being who has fallen so low that he is out of the grace of God. Maharishi Balmikii, who wrote Ramayan was a criminal in his earlier part of life. Many dacoits and wicked men have been totally transformed to good human beings with the grace of Guru in the past. It means that however fallen one is, even if to the extent of an ocean, it cannot be greater than the sky of the grace of God. The soul of one who falls low is in great pain and God will be more concerned about him, just like a mother (if she has three-four children) who will be more worried about the particular child who is either more unhappy or is sick. Anybody under the stars can follow any religion suitable to him and gradually, move towards God. Eventually, God will help him through a *Sadguru* or Master.

When Baba gives His grace equally to all, why cannot all devotees progress in the spiritual path equally?

Sadguru cannot leave His devotees under any circumstances whether the devotee realizes it or not. That is why Baba used to say that one should pray always to Him with *Shraddha* and *Saburi*. Whenever the grace of Sai descends upon anybody usually it is seen that his negative qualities reduce and good qualities grow. From those initial experiences only, some of the devotees think that they have reached somewhere in the spiritual plane or they have achieved spiritual knowledge. Taking this initial state of things to be the final state of achievement such people start behaving like Guru and collect disciples. Many people cannot progress because of this and try to live an artificial life. Those who conduct themselves in a normal way after receiving Baba's grace never exhibit the prowess of the devotion; they gradually achieve closeness with Baba. Nourishing spiritual and religious ambitions is a limitation in the path of spiritual evolution. Some people even after getting the grace of Baba to solve their problem again commit deliberate mistakes because of greed, anger or jealousy. Their growth gets delayed.

What are the traits of a perfect man and how to achieve this?

He who is completely liberated from all earthly entanglements is a perfect man. He is not limited by any place, group, system, laws of nature and has got full control on all base elements of mind, such as desires, lust, anger, etc. He is dispassionate under all circumstances and his vanity of being a man has also deserted him completely. Many sages who were proud in nature could evolve spiritually only when their ego was annihilated completely. There is the example of Vishwamitra and others.

Many people give us trouble. Should we not punish them?

Who are we to award the consequence to anybody for his doings? In the ultimate analysis this lies with God only. Everybody will bear the consequence of his or her actions. Many a times a human being misconceives himself of being the giver of justice to others in terms of punishments and rewards. Justice is delivered by God only. Because of our limited intellect we think that we are being subjected to injustice by somebody. However, in the ultimate reality, we don't understand that we had also committed similar injustice towards somebody in the past. Many times we become proud of our strength and capability and try to turn the situations in our favour with selfish interest. If one wields power then that should be used to conquer one's own self. If one wants to emerge victorious then one should conquer those causes due to which enmity and aggression arises in heart. No matter how much of hardship comes in life, one should bear the brunt of the circumstances or results of his actions with forbearance. It needs great amount of inner strength to be generous towards those whom we consider to be our enemies. Today, if we save ourselves from some aggression, tomorrow there will be a new set of aggressions. Thus, we will be left entangled in a cycle of cause and effect. If we punish someone today, he will punish us in next life. If we excuse, this chain of reactions also ends.

I think that I have surrendered to Baba. But then why am I feeling so much of pain? It is said that those who surrender to Baba do not get pain. But then why do I get pain?

Sadguru wants to liberate us. He wants to lead us to a place reaching where all our problems come to an end and a fountain of bliss begins to flow. But we are stuck up in the little thorny bushes of this path and get troubled by their pricks. We are not prepared to bear little pain a little more. We want that *Sadguru* should remove all such thorns, which cause us little little pains. One should not waste one's own and *Sadguru s* time with such thoughts. Why not hold on to the theme of devotion and forbearance in our heart and meditate at the feet of *Sadguru?* All our miseries will disappear gradually on their own. If our surrender is complete at the feet of *Sadguru* then we will not experience such pain. When a devotee is in pain, the Sadguru comes to know of it and tries to remove or neutralise such pain. Surrender to the Master reduces mental worry and the consequent pain.

When Baba resides within us then why don't we reach Him?

In the ultimate reality God, Guru, Atma are inter-related aspects of the same eternal consciousness. Baba is within us in subtle form in our soul known as *"Antarsakshi"* - one who knows everything about us as a witness. He is within us in the form of self- illumination. He creates noble thoughts in our mind. We do not have that power or inner sight which can see Him in the form of light. Yogis, after efforts of many lives get that inner sight by which they can see Baba's *Swaroop* in the form of light within them. Sometimes, we do experience Baba in our inner self out of the feeling of devotion and love but, we mostly imagine Baba in a mental form. We keep thinking of Baba's photo, words and His works. Moving ahead step by step we can reach His true form, when we become egoless, have no more desires, become totally detached, and take control over negative qualities like lust, anger, hatred etc. When our heart is pure and blemishless and mind is calm, then only Baba's actual form can be experienced. As the sky does not reflect on water when it is disturbed by waves, similarly, until mind is completely stilled and gets absorbed in the *Atma*, it is not possible to see Baba's form in it. One has to strive really hard for this. Only the *Sadguru* can instruct about that path correctly. Therefore, one should continuously pray Him and follow the commands given by Him to the best of ones abilities.

Knowingly or unknowingly, with the body or mind we commit many sins, can we control this?

Committing a sinful act knowingly and unknowingly are two different things. If any sin is committed knowingly it is certainly much more serious because we are aware that it is not right to do so but still do it. If we are walking on the road and an insect gets crushed under our feet or if we accidentally hit someone while driving on road, they are not so sinful acts as those done knowingly and consciously. The sins also fall into two categories - physically, by direct acts involving body and mentally, by thinking of sinful acts like, lust, anger, violence etc.

Very few people can actually understand what the final consequences of any of their actions will be because what is considered to be good today may turn out to be bad tomorrow.

We must pray to Baba that He should give us the capacity to discriminate the good from the bad. He should give us the power of judgment. We must pray to Him to take us from darkness towards light so that we are able to take just and right steps. We should read the life history of Saints to understand how they conducted themselves and how some ordinary human beings realized God by their faith, patience and self exertion.

We always seek for situations that give us pleasure. Is it proper to do so?

The concept is based on the distinction between 'pleasant' or 'unpleasant'. It is based on the Pleasure and Pain theory. It also limits our '*bhava*' and keeps us away from God, who is beyond all limitations and concepts. It is possible to realise that limitless and universal God by transcending these limitations of welcoming pleasant situation and avoiding unpleasant situations. When one evolves to the state of perfect mental equilibrium when facing both pleasant as well as unpleasant situations then he will come to know what God is. This is what one must strive to achieve. Factors creating happiness and unhappiness like the two faces of a coin are two facets of God. One must experience both to understand God.

We say that we are submitting our good and bad actions to Baba. At times knowing that we are committing a wrong deeds we do so. Why can't we stop such actions?

Despite all our efforts if we are not able to control our negative thoughts and actions then it could be the effect of cause or our *Samskara* carried forward from the previous lives. What happens spontaneously is predestined. For example, we don't want accidents to take place. Even then accidents do happen at times without any mistake from our side because the laws of *Karma* are inevitable. Our past *Samskars* or impressions which propel us to precipitate certain actions come from many births and they can only be removed through a protracted period of time. The Sadguru says that, "I have no

objections even if you commit mistakes a thousand times because I
know that you will commit mistake as you carry the impressions and
seeds of *Karma* through thousands of births. But I expect only sincere
efforts from your side to evolve in the direction of inner transformation
through a process of self analysis and honest actions. Go on trying as
I ask you to do. Through this process you will surely evolve." *Sadguru*
knows that His devotees are bound to commit mistakes. *Sadgurus* are
the incarnations of forgiveness, patience and peace. Therefore, their
grace is necessary for evolving out of such a situation through *Shraddha*
and Saburi as prescribed by Shri Shirdi Sai Baba. Through *Guru Kripa,*
we are sure to evolve.

What should be the state of our consciousness?

Our consciousness should be pure. If we really want to have direct
vision of the universal form of God then we should try to clean the
storehouse of old memories, experiences, thoughts, convictions from
our mind. Otherwise, in our consciousness in place of universality
limited pictures will be painted by negative and non-creative thoughts.

What is the difference between 'Paramhansa' and an ordinary human being?

One God realized Saint has said that the difference between
'*Paramhansa*' and an ordinary human being is as much as the difference
between a human being and a stone. The day man will understand
the difference between the two he will achieve the state of realization.
Through patience and sacrifice of a few lives under the direct guidance
of a Sadguru can one man from among a million reach the state of a
Paramhansa. Shri Ram Krishna of Bengal, Gajanan Avdhoot of
Shegaon, Shirdi Sai, Baba Tazzuddin and Akkalkot Maharaj - all were
Paramhansa.

If maya attracts everyone, then how to come out of its attractions? Does the Sadguru attract His devotees by the use of maya?

Behind this illusionary world i.e. *maya,* there is hidden the real form
of God. Till the time somebody, with the *sadhana* of many lives or
with the grace of Guru, penetrates through the veil of *maya* he cannot

understand the meaning and the reality of creation. The Sadguru attracts the devotees through the use of *maya* to make them experience both knowledge as well as ignorance. One should therefore surrender to the Master who only knows what is illusory (maya) and what is the reality in the world. As the grace of Baba increases, the shackle of maya also starts breaking down.

Can intellectualism become helpful in the Divine knowledge?
Our intellect is very limited. Originally, intellect functions on arguments. It is impossible to get any knowledge in the complete sense of experiencing it. Every human being has more of ignorance than knowledge, then how can he achieve complete knowledge?

In fact, direct knowledge comes gradually through one's own experiences. Without direct experience only a limited knowledge can be achieved. Divine experience is direct knowledge. It cannot be understood through an intellectual process as is done when understanding Mathematics or Physics.

I would like to know the definitions of innocence and goodness in Sai's view?
Read 'Shri Sai Satcharitra'. Innocence is a state of heart, mind and feeling. It has to be experienced. Observe a small child's behaviour. The more you read Shri Sai Satcharitra the more you will realize the truth. Baba always told and encouraged His devotees to be simple and truthful in all their dealings. Baba's approach towards all His devotees was simple and at times child-like. Behind all His actions was the inclination of helping His devotees.

My question is that why are the devotees of Baba in pain. Each one of them is suffering from some or the other kind of problem. Why are they suffering being so close to Baba?
All devotees of Baba are certainly not in pain. A real devotee of Baba will surely not consider the worldly pain as pain. He will consider his separation from *Sadguru* as a pain and would always try to be close to Him at the cost of the whole world. He is always in a state of ecstasy. Usually different people with worldly requirements and pain come to Baba. There is a small number who come to Baba out of love

without any problems. But Baba takes care of all of them. They are not suffering because they came to Baba. They are suffering the result of the past actions only. However due to the kindness of Baba their suffering gets neutralized and the power of tolerance increases.

Will not Baba listen to my prayer because I have committed some sins?

The prayers of all people whether they are saints or sinners are listened to by the Sadguru with equal importance. The Sadguru doesn't hate anyone because he has committed a sin or sins. On the other hand, He tries to render as much help as possible because He knows that a sick child needs more help. Continue to pray and Baba's kindness is bound to fall on you.

There are many noble people in this world who always help others, but still have to suffer a lot. Why does it happen while so many sinners live happily? Kindly answer.

Sinners don't necessarily live happily and good people do not necessarily suffer. This is over-generalisation. Past life actions at times create adverse results in this life for good people. Similarly for sinners of this life, at times good actions of the earlier life works positively. This creates the impression that you have. We should continue to be good with faith in Baba. Good results do follow ultimately in accordance with the "Law of Karma".

What is the Truth and what is God according to Sai Baba's view? Does Shri Sai guarantee to all His devotees that after they die they will go to heaven?

According to Shri Sai, God and Truth are the same. Only a truthful person can be divine. All these concepts of God, truth, heaven etc. can at best be pure intellectual understandings if one has not actually experienced the Truth. Baba certainly said that depending upon his good conduct or accumulated *Punya* (Virtue) one can experience the state of heaven.

To me everything happening in this universe seems to be so mystical and so systematic. Is it true?

Law of Nature is highly precise and scientific. Nothing is meaningless and unsystematic in nature no matter how small or how big – just as the atoms or the universe. To the human beings who did strive and knew the laws of nature, to them there are no mysteries. They are saints, yogis and Perfect Masters, that they could control the natural elements means they were well adept with the process of nature. It is true that nature, both at macro and micro-levels is organized as a system. There is no doubt about this.

All religions and particularly Hinduism, has from time-immemorial used different symbols for the understanding and expression of the multiple aspects of God. Since God is an attributeless Divine Entity, therefore, it has not been possible for the limited human mind to comprehend Him except through these symbols. Be it the conch of Hinduism or the star of David of Judaism or the holy cross of Christianity, a religious symbol not only gives an easy approach to God but also a manifested assurance to the devotees. The ancient Hindu seers had mastered over this symbolic representation of the various aspects of God.

Sai Movement

I want to start a "Sai movement" in a foreign land but have no idea or contacts to do that. How should I go about it?

First action to start a Sai movement is to make oneself mentally, morally and physically strong. The immediate steps you can take at the first stage are: -

a) Get His photograph, pictures for free distribution among other devotees.

b) Get books on Him and magazines for self-study and circulation.

c) Call the devotees on a Sunday and do prayer or *Aarti* of Baba.

d) To do Pooja of Baba or to meditate on Him.

Go step by step. Always pray to Him to give you the direction.

I have been hearing about a third world war by the end of the millennium. Is it true? What should I do to help spread the Sai faith?

Wars are bound to happen in any civilization. That is a much larger divine activity at a macro level. Till human learns to be tolerant and unselfish, wars will continue periodically. Dharma yudhas by incarnations like Rama or Krishna destroyed evil and encouraged righteousness.

To spread faith of Baba one should do whatever he is capable of doing - physical, mental, spiritual. The least one can do is to speak about Him, give His photographs, books and printed literature to others and inspire others to follow His path. There are many other ways one can imagine. Any needy person you help in the name of Baba is a good act. Even feeding or raring animals, birds etc. in His name is a positive act.

I am in search of my spiritual destiny at the moment. I would like to preach for Sai Baba but I have no resources for that. Please advice.

To have a desire to work for Shri Sai is a noble idea. But, at first one must create a ground to carry on such work through own hard work and patience. Such work can be done if one has pure emotions supported by intelligence, knowledge and material support. One has to create these assets for himself/herself before taking a plunge. The growth will be slow and one has to face this reality with forbearance. There is no shortcut to spiritualism. Pray to Baba to build you up for His cause.

What should be the role of patrons of Sai Temples towards the people who come to the temples?

The patrons should always work as facilitators to ensure that the devotees visit to the temples is comfortable and meaningful. Lot of hard work and planning is required to run the temples after the '*Praan Pratishtha*'. The patrons should work as a team to achieve this end. They should feel that they are like servants engaged by Baba to help the devotees. They should be polite, impartial and sensitive to needs of the devotees for whom the temple has been created. They should not give priorities to family members or relatives above the devotees in a temple.

Difference of opinion should not lead to difference of mind. Half the problems of our life will not arise at all if we remember this.

Experiences

It is said that Baba replies to any question that arises in our mind. I have experienced that. I get my replies through the books on Him. Is there any other way He answers our questions?

You are on the correct path. After reading books/printed materials on Him go on thinking and discussing with other devotees. He answers questions to us through our inner thoughts and in many inscrutable ways at times. Only the one who experiences knows. So at times it comes through dream and at times through the mouth of other human beings, unexpectedly. Shri Sai Satcharitra mentions about Dasganu Maharaj getting answer to his questions of 'Isha Upanishad' from the maid-servant of Kaka Saheb Dixit at his home in Ville Parle (Chapter 20 of Shri Sai Satcharitra).

All my life I have tried to make everyone happy and all I have got in return is sorrow. Why does it happen like this?

By doing good to others you are destroying your own "paap" and improving upon your qualities of forgiveness and patience and getting closer to Baba. Don't expect returns from human beings as you will get hurt. Expect it from Baba because in the right moment His blessings will descend. Pray to Baba always to keep you on the right path and to make you more patient. Please be true to your nature. All your virtuous acts are stored for future help. Don't change your helpful nature towards others.

I lost my husband in Leukemia about a year ago. My daughter and I prayed day and night to Sai to heal him and give him some more time. My husband was a good human being. He

even endured, first heart disease and then leukemia with great patience and courage. Why was he made to suffer? Why our prayers were not answered?

Before Baba left His body, devotees were requesting Him not to depart. Baba told that even He will have to leave the body one day. Any one born with a body will have to leave the body one day. The method of departure is pre-ordained because of past lives' actions called *"prarabdha"*. The ultimate answer can only be given by God. *'Karma prarabdha'* i.e. reactions to the actions done by one, is what the scriptures say the reason for all sufferings. Further, a certain amount of duty is given to a person within a certain period of time on this earth to complete. Once that is over he has to go. When the body becomes useless, by whatsoever manner to carry on the job for the jiva e.g. a diseased body, the soul departs and enters another body fit to do such work. This law of nature operates in the same manner on the good, the bad, the believers, the non believer and everyone equally.

I know your loss cannot be mitigated. But please continue to pray to Baba to give peace to the soul.

Is Sai Baba of Puttaparti, reincarnation of Sai Baba of Shirdi? That makes me confused.

In the history of mankind there never has been incarnation of an incarnation. Read books on spiritual science. You will get the answer yourself.

How much more do I have to suffer indifference of Sai who makes everything so difficult for me to manage?

Shri Sai does not make things difficult for anyone. He willingly took a human body to help us without seeking any returns from us. We at times, suffer the result of our actions of the past life or the present life. Please pray and have patience. Faith without patience does not give consistency in spiritualism. We cannot change the world which is so complex and ever-changing. We can change ourselves to adjust to the problems arising out of the complexities of the worldly life.

My belief in God increases when I'm in trouble. Is it a selfish behaviour or is it normal?

Human beings will always have problems in one aspect of life or the other, whether they are big or small, whether they are evil or good in nature. All such sufferings are correlated to *karma* of the earlier lives as also of this life. It is better to remember God more at happier times than when in sorrow, as Saint Kabir said "*Dukh main sumiran sab karen, sukh main kare na koi*".

What does the Sadguru try to do on His devotee and why?

In fact, Saints are both in the state of human beings and God simultaneously. In their past lives before their evolution they too suffered worldly sorrows like any ordinary human being. They gradually evolved to the state of a saint and experienced the divine world through hard work, patience and devotion to God. Having the experience of both the worlds, they can be the best advisors. However, they never advise people unless approached or asked and they never try to force their ideas on people. Those who follow their advice surely do get benefitted. Sadguru takes it as His prime duty to salvage the human beings from worldly miseries and give them *Sadgati* or liberation. He builds some devotees to become future Gurus as well to carry on His work.

Why do we want to test every experience on the basis of physical evidences?

Our intellect tells us to understand everything through the cognitive faculties. But our faculties are highly limited. The form of God is all pervasive. For direct experience a human being has to cross over the known and unknown boundaries of nature. Ordinary limited human beings can only see and experience the physical form. The yogis experience the subtler forms. One who experiences God's existence both in the seen and the unseen world is known as a *Jivanmukta or Paramahamsa*.

When one starts loving a Sadguru and establishes an internal contact with him, the divine love latent in his soul slowly comes out with all its manifestations.

Agony

I have known Baba's love and blessings for many years but since my mother's death due to cancer I have lost the ability to pray and feel as if nothing is going right for me. Could you please guide?

Love is the inner prayer whether outwardly done or not. Love for Baba is the greatest prayer because prayers are meant for evoking the love of Baba or God. Don't bother about formal prayers if the mind is in an unhappy state. Read and think about Him as much as you can. Your mother has gone because her time was over as ordained by the law of nature. Even Shri Ramkrishna Paramahansa the Sadguru of Bengal died of throat cancer. Pray Baba for the *Sadgati* of your mother and to bring stability to your mind.

I have been going through a very trying time and I feel that my faith is being tested. I have prayed for help and guidance, but I feel that Baba doesn't even hear me! I know that I am supposed to learn something from all this, but it is a very slow and painful lesson. How come I get no help from Baba?

The subtle but helpful actions played by Baba behind the scene for His devotees may not be known to the devotee at that time. Knowing the past karma of the devotee, the Sadguru quietly works on him in a manner which benefits him the best. One has to have steady faith and patience to reap the benefits of His blessings in due course of time, and at the time ordained by Him. That is why Baba qualified the word "Shraddha" (faith) with "Saburi" (patience). Either of these qualities cannot stand without the support of the other. If you read "Shri Sai Satcharitra" you will get your answers as Baba did answer these queries of devotees in His own way.

I have always failed miserably in my relationships because I tend to become over-possessive out of love. Will Baba help me to overcome such situations?

Love is above possessiveness. Love does not bind people to misery under emotional compulsions and manipulations. It is supposed to give more openness and understanding. Pray to Baba to give you the right direction. Our over-possessiveness in love is because of ego. Demands in relationships sometimes develop to unrealistic proportions, and then the problem begins. Further high level of criticality about the smallest mistake of the loved ones we have, are bound to be a futile exercise and adversely affects good relationships.

My husband is a very innocent person, but nowadays in this world innocence does not pay. Due to this his business gets affected. Please advise.

Both crooked and innocent people survive in the world. Both are the children of God and God has created suitable mechanism of survival of both the types of person. Nature has a scheme to balance the contradictory forces of nature. Thus the population of the deers has gone-up even if they are killed by tigers and the population of the tigers has gone down. Self-esteem is a virtue, which is not there with a pure soul. A contaminated soul may seem to prosper externally but internally he remains timid and afraid. Ask your husband to pray always, because Baba loves and protects the innocent persons. If one has decided to do business he has to face its gains and losses. One should accept both with equanimity of mind to get happiness in life.

These days I have trouble concentrating on prayers, evil thoughts come to my mind. It has been like this for a long time and I feel tormented. This could be the result of some bad impressions in this or some other life, but how can I overcome it?

The very nature of mind is to generate both good and bad thoughts. The basic instincts of a human being and also the accumulated samaskaras of his past lives tend to lead his mind astray even when he is meditating or worshipping. Our attempt should be to get out of such negative thoughts and focus our thoughts as much as possible when doing prayers or when meditating on Baba's physical form. In early stages of practice it is a mixed situation. However, with practice, prayer and faith in Baba such negative thoughts can be controlled. Whenever you have an evil thought please pray Baba to help -you control your mind and get out of it. Baba has clearly asked His devotees to remember Him when such evil thoughts raise their ugly heads. Sometimes such attempts give delayed result.

I am a devotee of Shri Sai Baba and know that He is always with me. Still I do many wrong things and feel guilty but I do not improve as I have a weak will power. How to overcome this?

The fact that doing anything wrong makes you feel guilty indicates that you love purity. Baba is purity personified and can control your mind in case you have full faith in Him. Continue to pray Baba and meditate on Him. Gradually, you will get over your weaknesses. Read life and teachings of Baba in "Shri Sai Satcharitra" and try to imbibe the pious qualities of head and heart which will make you pure and peaceful.

As and when I am about to commit any wrong deed why from within my heart Baba does not stop me from doing so?

The Masters like Baba operate as conscience in one's heart. You certainly hear your inner voice. Please take it to be the voice of the Master. Always focus your thoughts on Him and on your own conscience whenever you have any wrong thoughts. Please know that our Atma is our Guru and Guru-Shakti gives directions through the inner voice of the soul. We often neglect it due to other pressing compulsions of our complex worldly life. If we start practicing meditation, we will start listening to the inner voice.

"Kaal" or time is the most precious commodity in the life of human beings. Make optimum use of it in the most creative manner.

Materialism

Is being rich and having comforts of life, so called materialistic possessions, a wrong goal to attain? Does it take us away from God? Can we be closer to God even while concentrating on our materialistic progress?

God reflects through both material and spiritual aspects of human life. Who else than God has created the material world? The material aspect of life is necessary for the spiritual evolution upto a certain point. The examples of some of the Spiritual Masters show that they lived in the complex material world and yet evolved to the highest level of spirituality. Material world can be used as a medium towards spiritual progress. Being rich is not a sin unless richness is derived through sinful means and money is spent in sinful pursuits. Rise materialistically but use the material earnings for the cause of others to the extent possible by you. A rich man is the trustee of God to help the poor. If he distributes his wealth after keeping his share, he is doing the right job.

There is a tendency of some people to look-down upon the rich people as if they were all sinners of God. I have seen hundreds of cases of rich people being very pure and kind whereas I have seen lots of poor people quite dishonest. Hence one should not draw any conclusions.

> *Only realized souls know that the life under the protection of a Sadguru is much more joyous and meaningful than the so called life in the heaven, how-so-ever grand it may seem.*

Yoga

Did Baba teach yoga to His devotees? What were His views about yoga as we commonly understand?

Generally people understand yoga to be a sort of physical exercise with different Mudras and postures (Aasans). The details of yogic exercises are prescribed by Maharshi Patanjali, the ancient writer of "Yoga Sutra". Sometimes Pranayam (Control of breath) is added to it. Some people while doing meditation also sit in certain Aasanas like Padmasana or Siddhasana etc. Shirdi Sai Baba never prescribed any such yoga to any of His disciples. But he never spoke against it either. Some prominent devotees like Shri Upasani Baba, had gone through the whole length of yogic practices even before meeting Baba. Even when Shri Upasani Maharaj stayed at Khandoba Temple for more than three years, he was never asked by Baba to do such yogic exercises.

The various spiritual prescriptions given by Baba to different devotees, show that he believed in the purification, upliftment and control of mind. No doubt that many devotees when meditating on Baba were sitting in yogic postures, but Baba never advised anyone to sit in a certain posture and meditate on Him. His emphasis was always on the control of mind rather than on the control of body.

These days we find people practising yoga and pranayam through the televised yogic programmes. Common yogic exercises are prescribed to all viewers. Should everyone do the same exercises?

The system of yoga and pranayam are no doubt the best gift that the Hindu religious science has given to the world. Yogic exercises make the human body strong, flexible, long-enduring and disease free. The yogic exercises however are of two types. The first category of exercises is comparatively simple in nature and can be done by any person with normal health like Savasana, Sahajasana etc. However, for people affected by polio, paralysis or epilepsy etc. (either genetic or acquired in nature), specific exercises have to be prescribed by an expert. Further people suffering from specific diseases like Arthritis, Diabetes, Spondilysis, Asthma or diseases related to bones, muscles, tissues and even skin should not practise the yogic exercises generally prescribed for all. They should undertake appropriate exercises under an expert so that these parts of their body are not adversely affected. At times, many people are not even aware of the delicate condition of some of their inner organs like heart, lungs, kidney, liver, and intestine and particularly uterus in the case of women. If such persons start doing general practices without consulting a doctor or a qualified yoga teacher they are bound to get into trouble. Therefore, it is desirable that the yoga teacher should have good knowledge about human anatomy and pathology. Many yoga teachers that one hears of are actually not qualified even if they declare to be experts on the subject. Hence, before starting such exercises the practioner should read available literature on yoga and discuss the matter with qualified people on the subject. Everyone should not, cannot, and need not do all types of yogic exercises.

Should the people suffering from mental diseases perform yogic exercises?

Let me at the beginning differentiate between mental condition and mental diseases. At time people mix up the two. For example a woman crying hysterically in public view may be due to the death of a near relative. It is a mental condition and not a mental disease. Mental diseases are generally understood as psychopathic, psycho-neurotic and psychotic conditions of mind e.g. schizophrenia, paranoia, manic-depressive psychosis (genetic or acquired) etc. People suffering from such diseases should never start a yogic exercise without consulting the psychiatrist. In my view, Pranayam done under a qualified teacher is a better option for them. It can help in the stabilization of the breathing cycle which is vital towards maintenance of mental equilibrium. There is another category of people who are highly sensitive in nature and have less capacity to absorb stress and strain of life. Such people can perform specific yogic exercises which give them mental relaxation more than physical relaxation. They should avoid all methods of meditation, pranayam and yogic exercise which are likely to increase their mental stress.

The reason behind welcoming and celebrating a New Year, a New Century and a New Millennium is because human beings are always hoping for a better tomorrow keeping the past in mind. Tomorrow is a part of the time continuum in which every moment matters. If every moment and every day is spent in a creative, evolutionary and peaceful manner then human life becomes qualitatively better and joyous.

Astrology

In this mundane world full of complexities of life does a Sai devotee need to take the support of Astrology?
An astrologer can at best predict the future in a limited way. Whereas Sadgurus like Baba actually can help their devotees in the creation of their destiny. Once you have surrendered to Him He takes care, reduces pain and increases happiness and evolves the souls. Keep His teachings and life history in mind. See Him in happiness and unhappiness both. See Him in both mundane and spiritual matters. Allow Him to work on you by keeping Him always in your consciousness.

In this context it is worth remembering a story given in Chapter 22 of Shri Sai Satcharitra
A great astrologer named Nanasaheb Dengale told one day Bapusaheb Booty, who was then in Shirdi, "To-day is an inauspicious day for you, there is a danger to your life". This made Bapusaheb restless. When they, as usual, came to Masjid, Baba said to Bapusaheb- "What does this Nana say? He foretells death for you. Well, you need not be afraid. Tell him boldly "Let us see how death kills." Then later in the evening Bapusaheb went to his privy for easing himself where he saw a snake. His servant saw it and lifted a stone to strike at it. Bapusaheb asked him to get a big stick, but before the servant returned with the stick, the snake was seen moving away and soon disappeared. Bapusaheb remembered with joy Baba's words of fearlessness.

The Sadguru is like a tree that not only gives fruit but also fragrance and shade to all, even to enemies.

Ego

When and how one can control his "I"?

One who can take complete control over "I" i.e. ego, will not be born again as he would be merged with the Oversoul. Through the effort of many births, good deeds and grace of the Sadguru, one can get control over "I". False ego and pride etc are manifestations of "I". Ego can manifest in the form of 'Swabhimana' or 'Abhimana'. One must understand this and pray to Guru for release from this. By making life simple and surrendering it to Guru, -"I" diminishes slowly but surely. There are many aspects of ego like lust, hunger, anger, body, and mind. They get controlled slowly.

Baba always tells us that there should be no ego. Ego is a destroyer and kills the spiritual progress of a person. But, in our day to day worldly life one has to use his ego to establish himself in life. What to do?

Ego can both be creative and destructive. It is because of human ego that the biggest things are created on this earth and are also destroyed. To become ego less is the highest state of spiritual advancement. Baba has spoken the ultimate word. We, at a much lower levels of evolution can only try by taking His name. While doing a job where ego is necessary one should, always be careful not to demonstrate ones ego unnecessarily when it is not essentially required. Understanding the nature of one's own ego and then using it in the positive direction will not make a person the slave to his own ego.

While doing the work of Baba many obstacles come. Is this to kill the ego and also to instill patience and faith?

I entirely agree. The more work you do for Baba, the work of higher level will come to you, both quantitative and qualitative. At times big obstacles present themselves, but they do not remain for long. It not only kills ego but builds those qualities of Shraddha and Saburi that are essentially required to do bigger jobs for Baba.

When the Sadguru walks over the earth, the spiritual power in the planet gets rejuvenated. The Guru's shakti, positively effects all the living and the non living. The earth (Vasundhara) surrenders its burden at the Feet of the Sadguru for evolution of all the species living on it. Such is the Feet of Sadguru, where all surrender.

Fasting

I would like to ask why Baba did not prescribe or believe in fasting of His devotees.

No mother would like her child to fast for her cause. The Sadgurus like Baba are like mothers, who took care of their children without giving them the trouble of rigorous religious practices like fasting etc.

Fasting of the body alone is of no use if the mind is not fasting. What if the mind is thinking about worldly or negative thoughts while undergoing fast? On the other hand, if fasting of body alone could give spiritual or religious benefit, then so many people dying of hunger in continents like Africa and Asia, would have realized God. Poor people when dying without food or nourishment do pray God intensely to save them.

The concept of fasting in Hinduism is to prepare the body in the first stage to be disciplined and tough, so that it becomes an effective carrier for subtle energies. In case of *Bhakti Marg*, only self surrender to the Guru is necessary. He takes care of everything else including the body of the devotee. However, as prescribed in Hinduism if one undertakes fasting with a pious or spiritual state of mind it is all right.

> *When a man realizes God, then his consciousness expands to infinity. When the time limited concepts of a few years of human existence is seen in relation to the timeless activities of a Perfect Master, one evolves beyond the limitations of a small time period.*

Household Duties

How should a householder involve himself in the activities related to Baba while discharging his professional and family duties?

A householder has to take out time for Baba's work while discharging all the duties with perfection towards his family. His family life should be moderate and simple. If the lifestyle is kept simple, it can be handled easily. By organizing the daily routine of life try to minimize the time spent on it unnecessarily, so that more and more time is saved for Baba's work. The work related to the profession and duties should be organized in such a manner that while doing any such work the mind is completely free from the burdens of other things. This is possible only when one is properly organized. Whatever work you do concentrate on it completely at that time and finish it sincerely and properly. One should utilize his time for the smallest as well as the biggest duties with equal sincerity. Work should be attempted with a holistic approach because nature is holistic. If each and every action in life is done with faith, perfection and completeness then one can experience the closeness to God who only is perfect. Make Him your companion every moment while doing any work – mundane or spiritual.

How do I progress spiritually while doing my household duties?

Spiritualism and materialism always go side by side particularly for a worldly man. One cannot be put aside for the other because both are created by God. Observe Baba's subtle play in both these aspects. Both aspects have to be taken care of by following the path shown by Baba. Pray to Shri Sai, He will surely bless you. Total materialism limits the thinking and actions of a man. On the other hand Spiritualism leads to viewing the whole universe as a family – a single house. We pick up the qualities of love and co-operation from our own house and society, if we have a mind to learn. Performance of your household duties is necessary at this stage for the growth of your consciousness for your future evolution. It teaches you patience, sacrifice and cooperation with others.

How do I find solitude in this mundane world?

If one is not getting solitude even after trying hard it means that Nature or God or *Sadguru* wants him / her to experience living with others and adjust with the circumstances. We can always find solitude within ourselves, while traveling, before sleeping and immediately after waking up. Think of Baba at such moments and at all free moments you get wherever you are.

How does one take out time for spiritual evolution while staying within the limitations of an ordinary family life?

For human beings living an ordinary and routine life taking out time for conscious spiritual evolution has never been easy. Leading an ordinary life means following the accepted social, economic and religious norms prescribed and practiced from generation to generation and also to accept such changes that occur within its fold from time to time. Following the path of a yogi or mendicant is easy only for those who are prepared to shun the family life and social responsibilities and take to the ascetic path. However, it is a much greater problem to follow this path while carrying on a normal worldly life with family and social commitments. Most of the worldly devotees are, therefore, searching for 'Guru Path' as an easier solution to this problem. Once one accepts a Guru (a real Spiritual Master) it becomes easier to follow the path of spiritualism along with the worldly duties. The willpower of the devotee and the divine inspiration from the Master are the essential requirements for evolution under such circumstances. Herein the will of the devotee should be exerted to maintain a state of continued faith in the Master under all circumstances. In the first stage it is difficult to completely follow the path. It requires a number of years for preparation. If a man sets on the quest of a Guru, reading and thinking on the subject, particularly the life histories of Gurus, maintains purity in his conduct along with patience, gradually the divine thoughts of the Sadguru will grow within him. If he continues to do so, at a certain point of time he is bound to find a Guru who has the divine capacity to see-through the merits and demerits of everyone and read the thoughts of all His devotees. Therefore, it is said that the disciples do not find a Guru, but the Guru surely finds out His disciples. As Baba once said, "I draw My devotees from thousands of miles like a sparrow with a thread tied to its feet". In our life full of mundane difficulties and responsibilities, it requires great endeavor to develop the qualities of compassion, forgiveness and self-less service. Compassion and self-less service are the prime attributes of a Sadguru. Therefore at the initial stages one should begin with following the preachings of the Guru when rendering small services towards the Master and other human beings. Gradually one should move ahead towards rendering more difficult ones at the cost of one's own time and energy without expecting any returns. While undergoing life's struggle, whatever qualities one develops by his endeavor remain permanently within him and becomes a part of his jiva. These qualities are carried to the next life. In the next life also he gets the help of a Guru to evolve further along the spiritual path.

From the compound of your heart always keep clear the path going up to Shri Sai, so that whenever you are in troubled by the problems or life, you can find your way to Him.

Non-vegetarianism

I would like to clear the doubt in my mind as to whether Baba believed in philosophy of staying vegetarian? And if not, what logic was behind adopting non-vegetarianism?

Baba generally believed in staying vegetarian, but there is a mention in Shri Sai Satcharitra that Baba cooked non-vegetarian food for His devotees at times. In the ultimate analysis human beings have no right to kill any species for enjoyment, particularly, when they have been given the intelligence to know that God exists in every one including the species they intend to kill. Animals don't have this intelligence. This is Baba's basic preaching; but since all devotees cannot change overnight, therefore, they have to be handled differently. Simply being vegetarian or non-vegetarian does not necessarily make a man spiritual or otherwise. In the world more than 3/4 the population is non-vegetarian. Did these countries not produce spiritual leaders including Jesus & Prophet?

We should strive to be a vegetarian not only to avoid eating of flesh (even living vegetables have life), but because one should not be a party to the killing of other species. As per Hindu theory this *Karma* will affect him adversely. Besides, vegetarian food is easier to digest, particularly for the children, diseased and old people.

Is taking non-vegetarian food wrong or sinful?

No, because one creature will have to feed on another creature to sustain itself. But there are certain foods, which are natural, like the child who is nourished by his mother on her breast-feed. Human beings eat vegetables and after death their bodies are disintegrated and return to the soil and get absorbed by the vegetable world. But, killing an animal means we have separated the consciousness from us which had reached a higher level, and eating the flesh of a human means finishing the consciousness which had reached yet higher level than animals. Saints, who have reached a highly evolved state of consciousness, do not eat anything. Upasani Maharaj did not eat anything for one year. Some saints bring about such changes in their organic system that they can nourish themselves on the direct energy from sun.

Love and not hatred has ever brought or can bring peace to mankind. Shri Sai taught us that tolerance and sacrifice leads to love and love grows to divinity. Let us pray Shirdi Sai Baba, 'the incarnation of the Age', to give the experience of universal love to the human race, torn-asunder by hatred and conflict, today.

Anger

Baba did not like when devotees fought against each other at Shirdi. How can we take control over this anger?

It was not possible to extinguish anger even for a sage like Durvasa so easily. Many wise men and saints have also fallen prey to this. Anger comes from ego. If even a trace of pride is left in anybody anger may erupt whenever the pride is hurt. If one sincerely wants to get rid of anger he should think of Baba at the very first moment of anger and pray, "O Baba put off my anger". At that moment if the person who is causing anger is around then one should just walk out of that place and not indulge in arguments. Baba had said, "When two people fight with each other, I hold him dearer who is more enduring". This should be remembered consciously that, "Baba has said so, therefore, I will endure this anger". One should always nourish this thought. By doing this one can gradually find control over anger. It will take time to master such a feeling.

I tend to lose my temper very fast, how do I improve?

Whenever you get anger pray to Shri Sai Baba, and read His life history "Sai Satcharitra". Slowly anger will get controlled. Whenever you are angry with anyone, it is better to leave the place rather than quarrel Baba said that He loves those people more who are tolerant than those who fight. Regular practices of Meditation and Pranayam (breath control) can control anger. Reading of *Shri Sai Satcharitra* will also have a cooling effect.

> *Instead of conquering the world, conquer your mind. If you conquer your mind, you can conquer the world.*

Compassion

What is the reason that human beings want the feeling of compassion the most in God?

Human beings want the feeling of compassion the most in God, because people lack the power of compassion the most. We ask for something, which is lacking in us. God is "bhava", we are "abhava" i.e. lack of "bhava".

Are the humans compassionate towards the other living species if they want mercy from God?

This species called Homo sapiens has written so much of literature on against killing and harassment of other human beings and proclaims that God is in every 'Ghat' (living body). On the other hand, they are in the process of destroying the lives of other species. Killing of animals for eating, torture for enjoying sports (Bull fight etc) shows the lack of compassion in the human species. How strange that they ask God for mercy and protection, where as the animal world does not have that language to pray God.

If a man's heart is filled with the power of compassion then why should he ask for compassion from God? In that case he would reach the state of God himself. Divine compassion and grace is being showered continuously. It is necessary that one should have the worthiness in oneself and the ability to receive it. That comes from the evolvement of consciousness through lives. If human beings does not lack anything in life or if he gets everything he wants in life then he will not pray to God.

COMPASSION

Baba nursing the wound of a leper

Love of Animals

Baba liberating the tiger from agony and pain

What does Sai say about compassion?

Sai is the embodiment of compassion. He practised and preached the path of universal love which included the human beings and animals alike. He saw God in everyone and loved them and served them purely out of compassion. Read Shri Sai Satcharitra for the answers. He always encouraged and blessed acts of kindness. If you can't love you must not hate either. If one does not have the quality of compassion in himself, how can one receive the compassion of the Sadguru?

What type of human beings does Baba really love?

Baba is in the God State. He sees himself in everyone and hence loves all human beings and other species. Only if the quality of love is universally expanded in us shall we be in a state of heart to receive His unfathomable love. The more love we have in us, the more we experience Him. Ultimately, we will experience that Baba, God and we (our inner self) is one and the same thing.

The true service is to improve our qualities and be of some use to the causes of Baba, i.e. to serve the humanity around. BABA did reveal to some people that his divine consciousness covered even dogs, horses etc. Therefore, we should be equally kind to other specifies including animals and birds who live on this earth.

Charity

We see beggars in and around the temple or on streets, who we think resort to begging only out of lack of interest in working. At times I wish to help someone but a thought crosses my mind "is he actually needy?" Please advise me on this?

Every person is needy from his birth till his death. Everyone – be he a king or a poor man is a beggar before God. Everyone prays to God for something or the other. Baba said, anyone approaching us for anything is due to Karmik links of our past lives. By using your power of discrimination if you are convinced that a man is really needy then help him. In case of doubt, route it through Baba. If you wish to give ten rupees to a needy person but are in doubt then, put that in Baba's donation box in any temple. Let Baba decide this. In case you are not convinced at all then just refuse politely. As advised by Baba while doing so never abuse, threaten or misbehave with beggars. Don't develop negative thoughts about any one particularly the beggars whom destiny has punished enough.

In this world, so many innocent children in their tender age are subjected to various kinds of physical and mental harassment for the selfish needs of a few. How can an individual Sai devotee work to help those who are affected without sacrificing his professional and family commitments?

Every human being – child, young and old will go through a series of pains and pleasures. Please read "Shri Sai Satcharitra". Answers are there. It is because of bad actions of past lives that people suffer. One can always help these suffering children by rendering what-ever help is possible through donations, guidance, education, cloth food etc.

even without disturbing one's life. The compassion evoked in us is due to Baba that we are motivated to help. Where we can't, let us pray to Baba to help these unfortunate ones.

Many children are seen begging outside the temples. Should we not stop them from doing this?

From legal, social and medical points of view these children should be discouraged from begging. But, remember that these children do not beg out of any greed. It is generally a compulsion of life. They only wish that they should get some sweet, a piece of coconut or some money. They have such innocent looks on their faces. In spite of such poverty there is such happiness reflecting on their faces. There are greedy persons who pray or beg for much more after making lakhs and crores of rupees in the most sinful manner. For this they do all kind of crooked deeds. It is important that such people should change their mentalities. If we have the capacity to educate and look after these children we should do so. Without help they can't be stopped from begging except by law. But that is not a solution to this social problem which only society can solve. They need social security. In western countries such social security is provided by the society through its government. It is not so in India. So as social beings we should help them to the extent possible.

Sinners do not necessarily live happily always and good ones do not necessarily suffer always. Past-life's actions at times, create adverse results in the life of good people. Similarly, for sinners of this life, at times, good actions of earlier life fructifies positively. We should continue our faith in Baba.

Smoking

I am a smoker. I want to get out of this habit. But when I read Shri Sainath has also been smoker and offered the *Chillum* to others for smoking, I feel that smoking is not all that bad. Am I correct?

Baba was in a Beyond the body state (Videha) whom no material aspect including eating, sleeping or smoking affected. Saints at this spiritual height are Videha i.e. without the sense of having a body. They are pure spirits only using their body as a machine. By smoking and sharing the chillum with Baba, some people got cured of diseases, as mentioned in Shri Sai Satcharitra. His habit of smoking chillum and circulating among all devotees present near Him had a profound social significance. It dismantled social differentiation and ensured social brotherhood among His devotees at Shirdi. Through group *chillum* habits, He tried to break down the barriers between castes and religions. An ordinary person knowing the hazards of smoking cannot afford to continue with this habit for his pleasure only because it does not have a greater social significance. Further he will lose his health too. Pray to Baba to get you out of it.

Destinies are not comparable. Destiny of each person is unique in itself. So don't suffer by comparing and contrasting your destiny with that of others.

Peace

Please guide me as to how to stop worrying all the time and be at peace with myself.

Whenever you are worried think of Baba and remember His saying – "I take care of my children, no matter how far they may be". Divert your mind from the subject matter of immediate thought. Always think and assume yourself that the things which you thought would happen, never happened. Only that you wasted your precious time in worrying on them.

A man comes into contact with a Sadguru as a result of accumulation of lots of good deeds (Punya) in past lives. One can try to seek God by going from Guru to Guru but once the Sadguru comes to his life, he should end his search and surrender to him because He can only give God realization to the seeker.

Sex and Lust

I want to know whether taking interest in the sexual passions reduces our ability to reach God?

Sex is the most powerful, pleasurable and creative energy form in the living beings. Procreation and continuation of specie is the outcome of sexual inter-action between the male and female partner of that specie. This principle of nature is universally accepted by all societies, religions and scriptures. Sexual pleasures are necessary concomitant of the process of Procreation.

However, if it is overdone for pleasure only then it is harmful to the body, mind and the soul. Loss of maximum time takes place due to sex-related imagination, planning and activities. In such a state of mind it is difficult to concentrate and meditate on higher and finer concepts of God and Guru. Therefore strong sexual passions should be bridled. Pray to Baba to give you the strength.

Once when sitting near Baba in Dwarakamayee, Nana Saheb Chandorkar was attracted to a beautiful Muslim woman who had unveiled before Baba.

Baba spoke to him as follows – "Nana, why are you getting agitated in vain? Let the senses do their allotted work, or duty, we should not meddle with their work. God has created this beautiful world, and it is our duty to appreciate its beauty. The mind will get steady and calm slowly and gradually. When the front door was open, why go by the back one? When the heart is pure, there is no difficulty, whatsoever. Why should one be afraid of anyone, if there be no evil thoughts in us? The eyes may do their work, why should you feel shy and tottering?" (Chapter 49 Shri Sai Satcharitra)

What should be the attitude of human beings towards passion and lust?

As human beings we should keep our inner self in a pious and chaste condition. We must always remember the source from which all the *bhavas* emanate. It is much more important to be free of the *bhava* of lust than the act of lust. Some people are mentally engrossed in lust always imagining and wondering in their minds. Lust flows in their thought always and they commit number of such actions in a secret manner. Such people should keep their mind free of lust by taking along the Sadguru with them in their thought process always. Salvage your mind from those causes because of which the lustful *bhava* is generated.

Sadgurus or Qutabs or Perfect Masters or Masters who are in the 'jivan mukta' stage can only lead a man to God. All other Gurus, called by whatever names, can't lead a soul to God or to the Over soul. However, they can show the path towards God within their spiritual competence.

Life and Death

Do the non-living objects like stone, dust or metals have consciousness?

Consciousness as we understand do exist in living things like plants, fish, birds, animals or human beings is not there in stones, metals, water etc. However, before the living, the non-living elements like fire, air, earth, water and sky existed. Living aspects of nature like plants, birds and animals evolved out of the non-living. Therefore, living is non-living plus consciousness. When this plus factor called consciousness i.e. the life force goes away we cease to live. On death the consciousness merges with the universal consciousness as also the non-living matters merge with the elements of earth. Human body merges with dust and connects to physical / chemical elements. Therefore, it can be said that the primordial consciousness came in the form of non-living, later it took the living character.

Can there be life force any where else than earth?

Yes, Science is trying to explore it. But the Saints had already experienced the existence of life force and living organizers in other parts of the universe. Science will surely discover this in future.

Is there one universe or more?

There are innumerable universes. Like any living being, planets, stars and milky ways, the universes are also born and they also die through a certain process. The story of Lord Krishna meeting Brahmas (the Creator of universe) not only with four heads, but also with hundreds and thousands of heads is already there in Hindu Mythology. A single Brahmas represents a single universe.

Is there a past life? Did Baba believe in it?

Yes. If you read Shri Sai Satcharitra, you will find that Baba has spoken about the past lives of many people and His relationship with them. He has not only spoken about the past births of human beings but even of other species like frogs, lizards, goat and tiger. It is because of inter connected relationships of the past life that people come in contact with each other in the later lives. The payment made by human beings to settle debts of past lives called Rinanubandha creates happiness or unhappiness among them in the new birth. Baba has even referred to a lady Mrs. Khaparde as his sister in one of His earlier births. Unless we are prepared to believe that all our actions begin and end in one life and that there is nothing left after death, and also that there is no future life after death, then one question remains unanswered i.e. why did the most impartial, all merciful God, gave birth to people in different conditions and with different capabilities as a result of which some enjoy more and some suffer more. If there is no logic of such differentiation between human beings and other animals, other than the Karma Theory of the Hindus, then God cannot be seen as an impartial and all merciful entity.

Could you please tell us where our soul goes after death?

Soul is a subtle energy form. It remains in that form after death in the sphere of subtle energy. It is Atma. The body gets destroyed with death but the soul continues. It can take many bodies more.

What is life and what is death? Can one learn to leave body and experience death while remaining alive at the same time?

'Life' means a soul entering a body or creating a body and 'death' means a soul leaving the body leading to the destruction of the body. The Sufi's call such experience as *"jeetejee marna"* i.e. dying while living. It is possible through long practices and *Guru Kripa* alone. Sadgurus and yogis can leave their body consciously and return back to the body at their will.

What is the criterion of a soul being reborn as a dog or a blue whale? What is the end of the evolution of a soul?

God has multiplied Himself as a Divine sport and has created the universe. He enjoys seeing Himself in millions of forms on earth. Dog or blue whale or any other animal, are different manifestations of divinity in certain stage of consciousness and evolution. They go on evolving life after life till they reach the stage of human beings. Human beings ultimately evolve to the stage of Sadguru, the fullest manifestation of God Himself on earth.

Is it true that every soul has a mission in life?

Yes. Nature has already prepared a blue print of our lives. Just as human beings, within their limited intelligence, prepare blue prints before constructing a house etc. Every man has a mission to fulfill and each life on earth exists as long as the mission continues. The main mission of a Jiva with a soul is to evolve in every life till it finds its divine self.

What is the actual aim of life? What are we doing on earth?

The actual aim of life is to realize one's own soul or *Atma,* which is divine. Once one realizes this and have paid back our karmic debts, then he will not be born again. We are all experiencing worldly life, necessary to evolve us.

Do not ponder over negative thoughts as it is highly infectious in nature and gets into the system. Try to keep the negative thoughts out of your system as much as possible.

Sai Temple Inauguration – Dover
(UK), 27 Aug, 2001

Sai Temple Inauguration – Chicago
(USA), 19 Aug, 2004

Palki Procession Chicago
(USA), 19 Aug, 2004

Chicago
Temple

Sai Utsav, 22-25 Nov, 2000 –
Chicago (USA)

Devotees Adress, New Jersey (Nov, 200

Sai Utsav – Sydney (Australia),
9 June, 2001

Sai Utsav – Johannesburg (South
Africa), 27 April, 2002

Temple Inauguration – Chhattarpur,
New Delhi,
1-3 October, 1995

Temple Inauguration –
Injambakkam,
Chennai, 09 Dec 1993,
Ist Temple

Temple Inauguration –
Bhubaneswar 22-23 April, 1997

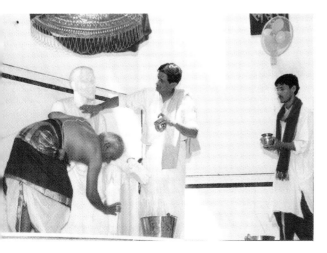

Temple Inauguration –
Noida Sector 61, (UP) ,
108th Temple 11-13
April, 2003

Interacting with Sadhus Maha Kumbh –
Allahabad (UP)
14 Jan, 2001

Ardh Kumbh – Allahabad (UP),
15 November, 1995

Ardh Kumbh – Allahabad (UP)
14 January, 2007

Ardh Kumbh – Allahabad (UP)
14 January, 2001

Garh Mukteshwar Mela – Moradabad (UP

Garh Mukteshwar Mela – Noida (UP)

...di Trip with Sai Devotees – 14-19 January 1999

Ardh Kumbh – Haridwar (UP)
22 January, 2004

...i Temple – Leper Colony, R K Puram,
New Delhi

Baba's Palaki Procession at Sai Ka Aangan
Gurgaon, Haryana

...rize distribution – Painting competition on
...ABA – Chattarpur Temple, 4th June 2000

Prize distribution – Sai Satcharitra and
Aarti test –
Chattarpur Temple - 4th June 2000

Samarpan Divas – Mumbai 02 Nov, 2008

Shirdi Sai Camp and Stall – Car Festival, Puri, Orissa

Inauguration of Shirdi Sai Public School,
Moradabad, 17 July 2003

Interacting with students of Shirdi Sai Public School, Moradabad, 2008

Group photograph of all students and teachers of
Shirdi Sai Public School,
Moradabad, 2008

Inauguration of Sai Vet Care – Moradabad (UP)

SECTION II : MESSAGES

The Sadguru not only raises the latent divine love in ardent devotees but also leads him in the most convenient and befitting manner towards God by himself removing all the obstacles that may come in the way of the disciple's evolutionary process.

Ram Navami Message 2009

The Absolute Consciousness or the divine form of the *Divine Player* is the real entity behind the manifestation, sustenance and transformation of this phenomenal world. Whether we consider the created world to be the reflection of God's unlimited intellectual brilliance and enlightenment or simply Divine Play, it is based on this Divine Consciousness, which manifests itself at different levels and in vivid forms. Everything that exists in this world, whether inanimate object or animate, object or not object (Vastu and Avastu) - all the species, existent or nonexistent, are amalgamated or embedded within the divine Super Consciousness.

Since pre-vedic times India's seers gave prominence to concentrating or meditating on "Tat Twam Asi" or "Thou Art That" or "You Are That." The evolution of civilization may also be termed as the evolution of consciousness. The pre-supposition of the creation of the entire phenomenal cosmos is borne of that 'Aham' or 'I' of that Divine One. However, this 'Aham' or 'I' is not the same as commonly understood, but it is the fundamental power which is the root of the process of creation. 'I am in everyone, everyone is Mine, and therefore, everything is within Me', this is what Lord Krishna preached Arjuna.

The human being is a very tiny particle of that Super Consciousness or the 'Absolute One'. Generally, his life is based on a very narrow thought process and he remains caught within the extremely limited boundaries of his self-centred role in life – himself, his family, his desires, his achievements, and that is all. Growth of God Consciousness occurs in the human being only when he expands his horizons beyond this limited boundary of his own and his family's needs and desires. Once this happens, his concern and sensitivity extend beyond himself and his family and include other human beings and creatures. Then the awareness of divine existence and power are awakened in him. This awareness enabled this small particle of the vast universe to contribute to become a part of the world creative process, the galaxies and even travel into and walk in space.

As soon as human concern and sensitivity, based on the power of love and power of desire, arises to work for the whole of God's creation, all conflicts come to an end and the jiva attains pure divine consciousness. This stage marks the end of the cycle of creation, sustenance and dissolution along the time continuum.

After transcending the concrete phenomenal world, the human being enters the world of *Vijñayan* or knowledge and then transcends the world of 'knowledge', he fully enters the world of '*Bliss*'. Then, the individual '*self*' exalts itself to a state of cosmic consciousness. After that is the state of *Paramahansa, Brahmastha, Jeevana-mukta Tureeyaateeta,* and *Trigunateeta* (the self emancipated from the bondage of the body despite being in the body) and then it will attain the state of *Sachchidananda,* i.e. the '*Real*', the '*Consciousness*' and the '*Bliss*'. Once this happens, the dialogue between Krishna and Arjuna in the Gita becomes meaningful, '*I* am in all, and all are *Mine*'. This is the real form of Sai Baba of Shirdi. Let us meditate upon Him all the time.

Experience God here and now! That is realization of God. Who knows what will happen after death. Hence, wastage of time means wastage of life and misuse of time means misuse of life.

New Year Message 2009

Shri Sai after Maha Samadhi

The very premise of worshipping a Sadguru or a Perfect Master is termed 'Bhakti'. The two major attributes of Bhakti, as defined by our Master Shri Sai Baba of Shirdi, are faith (Shraddha) and Saburi (Patience). The history of different Bhakti movements has shown us that the maintenance of steadfast faith in the Master is 'Perhaps' easier when He is in a bodily form and not as easy after He leaves His body. That is so because a Master in a human form can communicate and carry on with numerous visible activities over and above His subtle and invisible activities. When in a bodily form, the Sadguru can be communicated with by the devotees through the different cognitive instruments of the body (e.g. ear, eyes, mouth etc.) but the same is not possible with the Master's statue, photograph or painting. Those devotees who, during the period of human embodiment of the Master evolve spiritually and establish a subtle mental communication with the Master (even when physically away from Him), don't find it difficult to continue such communication with Him even after His taking Samadhi. However, those devotees who did not evolve when the Master was physically there or had never seen, heard, touched or smelt the Masters body or items (through the use of their gross physical instruments), find it difficult to maintain their devotion and faith as steadfastly as before, after the physical departure of the Master. There is a possibility of their devotion and concentration on the form of the Master getting affected gradually. The devotees usually get what can be termed, as a 'spiritual feeding' or 'spiritual vitalization' when directly in the presence of the Master. Once His body is entombed

(Samadhi), they worship the tomb not because of its aesthetic value but because underneath the tomb lies the body of the Master whom they continue to love.

For devotees who are born after the Samadhi of the Master, it is a different issue altogether. Their devotion emanates from the knowledge they receive from the old, experienced and direct devotees of the Master. They also get lots of information from the print media (books, magazines etc.) and audiovisual media (Movies, T.V., Radio etc.) about the divine personality, qualities and noble deeds of the Master. Today, they can get the requisite information through the medium of the internet. Thus when they start following a Master, they start reading the available literature on Him, asking questions about Him and participate in discussions on Him. Once influenced by the superior divine and humane qualities of the Sadguru they start worshipping Him. In this process, they establish a mental and emotional connectivity with the omnipotent spirit of the Master and also realize that the spirit of the Master even without a physical body can guide them in the path of spiritual evolution and protect them from worldly miseries.

However, there is another school of thought which holds that a Sadguru while in a mortal body alone can guide and protect His devotees. Once a Sadguru leaves His body, he cannot actively help His devotees. Therefore, they insist on following, what they call a "living Sadguru".

Let us take the case of our Master Shri Sai Baba of Shirdi. Before leaving His body, Baba gave certain assurances to His devotees in unequivocal terms, popularly known as the eleven sayings (Gyarah Vachan) of Baba. The gist of these eleven sayings is that, Baba will protect and guide His devotees (old or new) from His Samadhi, where His body is entombed. Once when in a mood of divine ecstasy, Baba made a forecast to a group of devotees that in the future, Shirdi would be visited by an un-imaginable number of devotees - both big and small - and they would make a bee-line to His tomb and also that He would be present in 'Guli-Guli' (correct pronunciation is Gali- Gali in Hindi which means 'every lane'). Let us examine whether Baba's forecasts have come true ninety years after His Samadhi (1918 to 2008).

During the last 90 years and particularly during the last 20 years or so, the spread of the name and fame of Sai Baba and the increase in the number of His devotees is phenomenal. There has been a mushrooming growth of temples and other related activities (medical, educational, social and religious) in the name of Baba all over the country and abroad. The number of books, magazines, souvenirs etc. created exclusively for spreading the name and preaching of Baba in different Indian and foreign languages is too numerous to be listed herein. Not only are hundreds of new temples coming up all over the globe, but also in many existing temple complexes, His statues and images are being consecrated. Television channels and internets etc. are regularly displaying various shows of His life and His preachings. Many devotees are experiencing His kind divine intervention in times of distress as a result of their prayers even today. Thus, the 'Sai Movement' is an intensely dynamic process that is flowering and prospering day by day.

This naturally leads to the belief that a Sadguru or a Perfect Master is as potent without a body as He is with it. Therefore, the devotees of Shri Sai Baba of Shirdi do not have to lament that they could not experience the physical presence or the divine activities of the Master when He was in His mortal embodiment. He is omnipresent and omnipotent and the mere lack of a physical manifestation of His power need not make His devotees lose faith and hope. Baba had promised His devotees of protection even after leaving His body and He has kept his promises as His devotees feel.

On this New Year, I pray Shri Sainath Maharaj to bless the millions of His devotees, grant them health and happiness and lead them on the path of spiritual evolution. May the year 2009 bring them closer to Baba.

The brightness of the worldly pleasures blinds people so much that they fail to see the light of God.

Dussehra Message 2008

The Theory of Karma as Propounded by Sai Baba

In chapter 47 of the "Shri Sai Satcharitra" written by Late Shri Govind Raghunath Dabholkar (Hemadpant), there is a story told by Shri Sai Nath Maharaj to one of his devotees. Baba had given out the story as His own experience with two characters – Veerbhadrappa (a snake) and Bassappa (a frog) with whom He had relationship in their past lives. As the story goes, Baba once heard the painful sound of a frog, when He was moving in a village. Being moved by the painful sound He searched for the frog and found him on the river shore and saw that a snake was trying to swallow it. Baba had divine capabilities of knowing the past, present and future of all those who came in contact with him. On seeing the snake and the frog in the situation of deadly animosity, He tried to separate them by reminding them of their inimical relationship in a past life. Baba told the snake i.e. Veerbhadrappa, that he and the frog Bassappa had killed each other in the past life as the result of a bitter rivalry. As a consequence of their evil deeds, they were re-born in the form of a snake and a frog and since their evil thoughts against each other had been carried forward to the present life, they were unconsciously propelled to restart the past antagonism in such a manner. He advised the snake to let go of the frog so that the seed of enmity between them brought forward from the past life is not further carried forward to the next life. Listening to what Baba said, Veerbhadrappa (the snake) released the frog (Bassappa) who jumped to the river and escaped. This depiction is in the style of a beautiful parable told to children in Hindu folklores. However, an in-depth understanding would reveal that Shri Sai Nath

Maharaj was propounding the basic tenets of the Karma Theory of Indian Spiritual Science.

One important principle of the Karma theory is that the reactions of actions (good and evil both) committed in the past lives are bound to come into play in the next life (or lives). Those with whom one had good relationship in the past life will be friends in the next lives and those with whom one had bad relationship in one life will become enemies in the next lives. The second principle is that the law of nature through its unseen ways of working will bring them together and precipitate the good or bad events as ordained from the past life. The third principle is that due to the play of "Maya" (Human Illusions created by the laws of nature) such human relationships will be established in the form of any social relationship e.g. friend – friend, brother – brother, husband – wife, master – servant, father – son, lover – beloved etc. Such relationship can even be extended to a human being – animals / birds relationship or animal – animal relationship. Baba was categorical in making the statement that no one develops any sort of a relationship with another person unless a relationship had not been brought forward from previous life (lives) even if one is not aware of his past lives. In our daily life we at times experience that the much desired or admired social relationships sometimes lead to unpleasant /acrimonious events. We also experience that sometimes person(s) with whom we have had no family /social relationships become best of our friends. History is full of such instances of bitter animosity between fathers and sons, brothers and brothers, husbands and wives leading to a miserable state of existence and mutual destruction. Think of the stories of kings Ajatashatru and his father Bhimbisara and Aurangzeb and Shahjahan. Unless something is done in the current life of the individuals to end this continued state of antagonism, it will spread over few lives more.

Shri Sai Nath Maharaj therefore prescribed to the snake and the frog that they should not indulge in further actions of rivalry and that they should wipe-out the evil thoughts towards each other in order to burn the very seed of antagonism. This is what most of the spiritual masters like Lord Buddha and Christ preached and practiced themselves. In short, the principle is to "Forgive and Forget". Many people try to practice this principle as advised by the masters in their life. Nevertheless, problems arise and the best benefit doesn't accrue to them due to limited or partial understanding of this concept. In a set of relationships people mostly try to adjust because of certain social /economic compulsions and forgive the actual or perceived injustice which they think has been committed against them. Some people at times think that they have forgiven when actually they haven't. The act of forgiving can never be complete without forgetting. Such acts of forgiveness can at best be termed as temporary solutions because usually in unguarded or stressful moments the old negative thoughts re-appear with double vengeance. It is difficult to forgive others when one thinks that he is totally correct or is less blameworthy than the other person who is totally wrong or mostly blameworthy. It is more difficult for the person whose memory is more intense and long lived to re-adjust /forgive his actual or perceived adversary.

It is easier for simple, egoless or light hearted people to clear the feelings of hurt and naturalise / normalise the course of their life. The more the grudge one carries against someone, consciously and sub-consciously, the more miserable he becomes, cloistered in the cave of his memory. Psycho-analysis reveals that if one person intensely and continuously picturises another person as his enemy, the other person, even if he is not his enemy, will gradually develop adverse feelings towards the originator of such negative thoughts. This is the most common method of creating enemies through our sub-conscious thought process. Similarly by generating positive thoughts towards others one can create friends. "I can forgive, but I can't forget, is only another way of saying, I will not forgive. Forgiveness ought to be like a cancelled note – tore in two and burned up, so that it never can be shown against one" – Henry W. Beecher. And Mahatma Gandhi said "the weak can never forgive. Forgiveness is the attribute of the strong".

In view of what has been stated above one cannot but agree with the prescription of Shri Shirdi Sai Baba given out to His devotees while narrating the story of Veerbhadrappa (a snake) and Bassappa (a frog). The only way to get mental peace and evolution in life is to control the negative thought processes generated in our mind so that one doesn't create further negative 'Karma' which one has to suffer in the same life or the next chain of lives. May Shri Sai bless us all to get out of our negative 'Samskaras' reflected in our thoughts and consequential activities. Jai Shri Sai.

Guru Purnima Message 2008

History has shown that the Divine Incarnations (Avataras), Perfect Masters (Sadgurus) and other spiritual personalities are capable of bringing about great and long term social, political and other changes at different places and at different times on this earth. Some of them like Lord Buddha, Lord Christ, Prophet Mohammad and Guru Nanak were instrumental in creating new religions as well. Some others Prophets have shown new paths for betterment of the human race and spiritual evolution of the souls coming into their contact with them. When they carry on their Divine and universal duties as ordained by God the Almighty these spiritual entities are automatically supported by the mighty and unseen powers of nature. The possession and use of such powers is natural to them. These powers are far superior in nature to the powers that all others species, including human beings, possess. These are called 'Divya' (Divine) powers or Siddhi (ocult) Powers. From the word 'Divya' comes the words 'Devata' in Hinduism. While working in a human form these spiritual entities are capable of displaying the powers and characteristics of both the human beings and the Devatas as per their will and requirement. Just as the human beings have superior power and intelligence over all the other species on this earth, so also these powerful divine personalities possess far superior intelligence and vast capabilities much beyond the capabilities of human beings. Just as a man does not always have to think that he knows veterinary or medical science when treating an animal, similarly these Masters are not aware of their divine powers when they are helping or treating human beings and other species whether in their worldly problems or in their spiritual evolution. They use these powers spontaneously for benefit of others without expectations of any material returns. It is their magnificent quality of kindness that propels them to help others and suffer for them. On the other hand, human beings, when they come face-to-face with such a mighty personalities are utterly surprised and moved to see the miraculous play of spiritual powers. Further, the kindness with which Masters use these powers for their benefit of the devotees and destitute brings forth an emotional upsurge in their hearts. This is beginning point of Bhakti. This is what used to happen to anyone and everyone who came in contact with Shri Shirdi Sai Baba when He was in His human embodiment at Shirdi. Baba's capabilities to give immediate and long-term redress to any problem of any person (both temporal and spiritual) was so vast and effective, that even the most powerful and capable personalities of that time like Dada Saheb Khaparde, Shrimant Buti, Kaka Saheb Dixit, Nanasaheb Chandorkar etc. looked insignificant before Him. Forgetting their material or social status they had to surrender at the feet of this kind Master. Being totally overpowered by the personality of Shri Sai Nath Maharaj and deeply indebted to Him for His kindness, these devotees started spreading His glory wherever they went. They spread the name of Baba mostly through the word of mouth and through varied social interactions, whenever they got a chance to do so. Ardent devotees like Dasganu Maharaj spread His name in the rural areas of Maharashtra through kirtans, ballads and folklores.

During the period when Baba was at Shirdi (1860-1918), there were a very small number of newspapers and journals in Maharashtra. Study of such newspapers and magazines shows that during that time, Baba's name rarely appeared in them. After Baba left His body in 1918 "Sai Leela" an official publication (magazine) of Shri Shirdi Sai Baba Sansthan came to existence and this continues to be published till today. The prominent devotees of Baba like Dasganu, Chandorkar, Kaka Saheb Dixit and many others who were instrumental in spreading the name of Baba were extremely cautious and truthful in uttering or writing anything pertaining to Baba. The two magazines, Sai Prabha (1915-1919) and Shri Sai Leela (1923 till date) were not commercial ventures. Neither the publishers, nor the editors or the writers had any commercial angle attached to it. It was out of pure love towards Baba and the real life experience they had with Him, that they published their experience in these magazines for the benefit of other devotees. They did not brag about the information they shared with Baba or their proximity with Baba. They did not write stories on imaginary / concocted miracles purported to have been done by Baba. They did not indulge in bringing out competitive marketing serials based on half baked truths or speculations on Baba, as is sometimes being done in audio/video channels of today.

Today nine decades after Baba's Maha Samadhi, His name continues to spread far and wide in India and abroad. As per Baba's forecast, today Shirdi is thronging with devotees coming from all over the globe and the number is ever on the increase. Hundreds of temples have come up in His name in India and abroad and more are in pipe-line. The number of commercial movies, TV serials, magazines, books, audio-video cassettes pertaining to Baba in different Indian languages is too numerous to be listed. Stories on Baba's life, news and views on activities pertaining to the Sai movement today and experiences of devotees can be seen through these audio/video/ print medias. Some of them are good. However, what is sometimes lacking is a truthful and correct projection of Baba after carrying on due research on the subject. Some people are perhaps not aware of the fact that a real Spiritual Master like Baba does not need a purely commercial venture to attract His devotees towards Him. By their subtle divine power, the Spiritual Masters can draw any soul from any distance by their sheer will. This is what used to happen at Shirdi during Baba's time. Baba has clearly mentioned that He can draw His devotees even from beyond the seven seas whenever He willed. A true devotee who has full faith in Baba would avoid projecting Baba through imaginary or concocted stories of miracles. Such false projections send a wrong message to the devotees and works as a hindrance in the correct appreciation of the personality of the Master, His philosophy and His teaching methods. Otherwise also, Shirdi Sai Baba, even after leaving His body about ninety years back is a living and helping divine force for His devotees.

On this day of Guru Purnima the devotees should pray the Master to give them the correct emotional and mental capabilities to understand Him through their inner perception. The devotees should not condition their mind through whatever they read, see and hear superficially about Baba but should read Shri Sai Satcharitra regularly and concentrate on the divine attributes (qualities) of Baba and meditate on His form. Only then can become the worthy ambassadors of their Masters and carry out His divine job.

Ram Navami Message 2008

Devotees of Baba may remember that on one occasion, Shri Shirdi Sai Baba advised one of His devotees working as a Magistrate, to maintain 'probity' in personal and professional life. The word 'probity' means a high standard of moral behaviour or adherence to the highest principles and ideals or in short, uprightness in whatever one is engaged in doing. People from all walks of life, such as government servants like magistrates, revenue officials, tehsildars, mamlatdars, police officials to lawyers, artists, pilgrims, used to flock around Baba at Shirdi, seeking His divine blessing, help and guidance, both mundane and spiritual. Baba helped everyone as per his need, without any considerations of religion, caste, creed, temporal status or varied social differentiation.

Of all the advice that Shri Sainath Maharaj rendered to His devotees, the most important and common advice was to maintain uprightness and honesty in all aspects of life religious, social, professional or personal. By asking the Magistrate to exhibit moral conduct in his profession, Baba gave the message that demonstrating the quality of righteousness in only one sphere of life i.e. in religious activities only, is not conducive to spiritual growth of an individual. It has to be practiced or adhered to in every sphere of life. It has to be a holistic approach. It has to be in the personality of the seeker to be righteous and truthful.

In our ordinary life, we come across many people, who demonstrate the quality of piety by donating lots of money to the temples, but shirk away in rendering any such help to their poor domestic servants, even if he or she may be in dire stress due to any reason such as the sickness of his or her child etc. There are others who spend lots of money and time on the rearing of their pet dogs, but do not think twice before hurling abuses and even beat up urchins begging on the street. Such examples are too numerous to be described within the limited space of this article. Such people show contradiction between their thought and action, where they display their virtue selectively and at times simply for mere personal gain. Thus, the qualities of uprightness, probity and honesty are applied as mere utilitarian principles and not moral principles as Baba had prescribed. One need not be surprised at such examples, because to be successful in the worldly life of today, most people take recourse to such a formula. However, such an approach is not conducive for those who are desirous of inner evolution. The formula that Shri Sai Baba of Shirdi prescribed, was to uphold the qualities of tolerance, compassion, uprightness, sacrifice and non-attachment and to practice these resolutely in every sphere of life be it professional, personal, religious or social.

Those who followed these preachings of Baba in letter and in spirit gained spiritual progress at a much faster rate than those that did not follow. Shri Sai Satcharitra cites stories of many such evolved souls during Baba's lifetime, such as, Megha, who maintained his qualities of truthfulness, faith and simplicity till his demise, Bala Saheb Bhate and Kaka Saheb Dixit who renounced the worldly life entirely on the bidding of Baba, while Mahalsapati maintained his non-attachment to materialism, till his end. These exalted and noble souls, and many others, who never faltered in sustaining their moral principles in life under the guidance of the Master of Shirdi, have been praised in Shri Sat Charitra and elsewhere.

Therefore, it behooves the true Sai devotees to consciously try to improve upon and evolve the best qualities in them; and put them in practice in all the activities they undertake. No doubt, this is not an easy thing to achieve, but steadfast love, devotion and unwavering faith towards Baba gradually brings out the best qualities in them. May Shri Sai bless us all, to be able to follow the path of righteousness and uprightness.

A number of Judges, Magistrates, Police officials, Revenue officials, Advocates and rich businessmen were Baba's devotees. Nanasaheb Chandorkar, Shri Hari Vinayak Sathe, Baba Saheb Bhatte etc. were Executive Magistrates, Shri Rege was a judicial magistrate who was elevated to the status of a High Court judge (Posted at Indore), Dada Saheb Khaparde and H. S. Dixit (Prominent lawyers who fought cases in favour of Bal Gangadhar Tilak), Shrimant Buti, the richest man of Nagpur, Das Ganu a Police officer and many other persons of such prominence were the ardent devotees of Baba. Their official activities were vital for the welfare of the society in which they used to operate. If they were corrupt and insensitive people, then the justice they were supposed to give to the general public would have been defective and harmful for the social good. On the other hand, by committing sins in being unrighteous, they would have added to the 'Papa Bhandara'. Thus it would have been a peculiar situation when Baba the Master would be trying to cleanse the negative and unrighteous qualities of their minds, but they trying to continue to with their unrighteous practices and yet loving Baba. It is to take out of such conflicting situation that Baba used to advice and even force them to maintain the qualities of probity and uprightness in public life.

For the devotees of Baba living in today's world full of corruption and greed, it may be difficult to be absolutely honest in the personal life while adjusting with the society. However, they can and should try to maintain as much steadfastness and probity in their professional life as possible. While doing so, they may have face with some opposition from the dishonest one's, but my experiences in life convinces me that if one continues to pray Baba when holding such high standards of conduct and character, finally he will succeed ad everyone will respect him. The devotees of Baba should never fail in such moral values.

New Year Message 2008

The religious and spiritual works of Hinduism has produced an unimaginable large volume of books, treatises, scriptures and other similar texts. Carried from the distant past are the most profound religious scriptures like the Vedas, Brahamanas, Puranas, Samhitas, Upanishads, Shrimad Bhagwata Mahapurana (which contains the 'Gita' etc.) and many more, too numerous to be listed here. A study of these works, written primarily in Sanskrit or in other vernacular languages will lead one to experience a sense of expansion in one's knowledge, imagination and consciousness hither-to unknown to him.

From an academic point of view, these valuable scriptures deal with spiritual philosophy, spiritual theory and spiritual science. In their quintessence they propound certain vital theories/concepts of the spiritual realm. Understanding of philosophy and theory are the first and basic requirement for a spiritual practitioner. However, it needs to be clearly appreciated that a mere study of spiritual and philosophical discourses is not enough. Any knowledge, which is not put into practice, shall not be of much use as the path of spiritual progress calls for direct experience and knowledge. So it is necessary for the spiritual practitioners to graduate from the mere understanding of spiritual theories to practicing the applied aspects of the spiritual science. Raja Yoga, Karma Yoga, Gyana Yoga, Laya Yoga, Bhakti Yoga, Hatha Yoga and tantras etc. deal with the applied side of the Spiritual Science.

How does one achieve spirituality? As mentioned before, merely by reading spiritual or religious texts one cannot spiritualise oneself. In its generic sense, the word 'spirit' here in means an indestructible divine energy form whose continued and unlimited play, sets into motion a series of changes in all forms of existence including the human beings, starting before its birth and going beyond its death. Different people understand the word 'spirit' differently. Some term it as called 'jiva' (living entity), some term it as 'prana' (life force in the living being), some call it as 'chetna' (divine consciousness) or 'atma' (a part of the ultimate reality called God or Brahama). These four words, jiva, prana, atma and chetna are intrinsically related. However, 'atma' is the primordial causative factor, of chetna, jiva or prana. In a way it can be said that, a continued state consciousness beyond time and space is the very nature of the 'atman'.

'Paramatma' and its part Atmas are the essence of the divine creation; they are the 'ultimate realities' beyond time and space. The cosmos is nothing but a manifested form of the 'paramatma'. Therefore, each created object in this universe contains a subtle and small part of the 'paramatma' termed as the 'atma'. Since 'atma' is a part of 'paramatma' it contains all the attributes of the 'paramatma'. It is omnipotent, omniscient and omnipresent in an unfathomable time continuum like the Paramatma.

So then, what is God realization? The word 'atma sakshatakara' (God realization) means, realisation of one's own 'atma' or consciousness. Even though these particles of 'paramatma' called 'atma' may be functioning in a 'Jiva' yet it is never separate from its root, that is 'paramatama'. Therefore, the realization of God is not the understanding of the material manifestation of 'atma', which includes all the living non-living and visible and non visible things and forces existing in the Universe. Even if one can travel to all the Universes in space and gain knowledge about it, yet he cannot be said to have realized God.

Different types of consciousness seen in its varied form seen on the earth emanates from 'atma' or soul or 'paramatma'. All forms of energy in the Universe emanate from consciousness, and all forms of materials emanate from those different types of energies. Thus, consciousness is superior to energy and energy is superior to matter in Universe. Whereas consciousness can explain and control all energy and material forms, however, the reverse cannot be true. Therefore, all religious worships of any deity in any form may not necessarily spiritualise a man. Any experiment in the spiritual science, means expansion of ones own limited consciousness to the State of a Universal Consciousness. That science through which the human consciousness can thus be evolved is called 'vigyana maya jagata' or the world of the spiritual science. To achieve this he has to introspect (dhyana) on his own conduct and thought processes continuously. Idol worship, mantras and rituals are prescribed procedures at the beginning to purify oneself. Once the mind is purified through the control of senses the consciousness slowly starts expanding. There is no short-cut to this.

If one studies Sri Sai Satcharitra, one would find that the actions of Sri Shirdi Sai Baba reflected this Universal Consciousness. To evolve spiritually, we should therefore try to follow his precepts and conduct in letter and spirit.

Om Sri Sai

Dussehra Message 2007

Often during my visit to the temples of Shirdi Sai Baba and also when attending the functions relating to Shri Sai Baba of Shirdi, I at times observe certain types of conduct of devotees as also the general visitors to the temples, which to my mind does not seem appropriate for the place or the occasion. Far to speak of higher spiritual senses and sensibilities, even the common sense of an ordinary man would dictate that certain dress and behavioral codes are required to be adopted in a certain situation. Let us think of a few such situations i.e., a marriage party, an official conference, a funeral procession and a golf tournament. Can anyone think of attending a marriage party in an attire meant for playing golf or an official function in the attire befitting a funeral procession? The dress codes prescribed for each of these occasions are different. Such dress specifications have evolved gradually over a long period of time in human civilization, because they are appropriate to the occasion. The idea is to maintain an environment comfortable for all and also to take into consideration the sensitivities of other human beings around. Since to be civilized means to compromises and accommodate the sentiments of others, it is essential that while in a place meant for group activities particularly in a temple one must be dressed appropriately.

Now let us examine the way the devotees of some religions dress or conduct themselves while in a religious congregation. While in the church the Christians are fully and appropriately dressed. So also is the case of Sikhs, Muslims, and Buddhists etc. When inside a place of worship the devotees are supposed to concentrate all their faculties for a definite purpose and in a certain manner i.e., eyes (through which they concentrate and meditate on the image of the deity), mouth (through which they recite mantras or *aartis* and *bhajans* in praise of the deity), ears (through which they listen to mantras, *aartis,* discourses etc.), nose (through which they smell the sweet smell of flowers and incense offered to the deity) and skin (through which they touch the feet of the deity). One can imagine the serene atmosphere of a temple, which gives a feeling of expansion of mental horizons and upliftment of the soul and an ecstatic mood. The most desirable atmosphere in a temple is a situation where one can listen to the prolonged somber notes of the Vedic mantras, there is no hustle bustle and no high pitched and abusive ruckus. The temple or the place of worship should also not give a picture of a depressed and melancholic with sulking devotees vitiating the whole atmosphere with their never ending demands from the Lord. Such devotees, creating scenes in the temple due to non-fulfillment of their purely material desires spoils the pleasant and peaceful atmosphere of the temple. The place of worship needs to be a place of unison of minds and souls of devotees, when focusing on a deity, or when chanting mantras and also when singing the *aarti* together. When the purpose, the thoughts, the sentiments and the activities of the devotees are merged in invoking the Deity or the Master, the love of the Master or Deity flows down to the devotees. This is the purpose and the method of going to a temple or a place of religious congregation.

When such a pristine atmosphere is about to raise the souls of the devotees to a state of sublime ecstasy, any sort of impropriety in dress and conduct such as talking or laughing loudly by a devotee knowingly or unknowingly is likely to disturb the other devotees and vitiate the whole atmosphere. The focus of the devotee is now shifted from the Deity, and in our case, the holy image of Shri Sai Nath Maharaj of Shirdi towards such individuals enacting undesirable scenario in the temple.

Shri Sai Baba of Shirdi was never in favour of his devotees and workers wearing any sort of gaudy clothes when taking part in religious ceremonies. Once Maharaj *Dasganu* the famous ballad singer on Baba and other saints came to Baba on his way to a religious function, where he was supposed to give a rendition of songs on Baba. He was donned in a dazzling and colourful attire, which *Kirtankars* and *Kathavachaks* usually wear in Maharashtra and elsewhere in India. Baba asked him not to decorate himself in such lavish style and attend the function in the simplest possible dress. (This incident is given in Chapter 15 of Shri Sai Satcharitra.) Following the dictates of the Master, thereafter, Dasganu always conducted the Kirtans wearing a simple Dhoti.

In the light of what has been explained above, it is desirable for the Shirdi Sai devotees to worship Baba in the temple or to participate in a congregation of devotees in modest and simple attire. Baba's teachings show that lavish display of material aspects of life including dazzling dresses were not conducive to a spiritual life. Shri Sai Baba, the Fakir with the torn and tattered clothes perhaps finds it more comfortable to be with His simply dressed but truthful people.

In this context I have also observed many devotees trying to wear clothes in the style and manner of the Master, wearing *Kafnis* (long flowing cloth covering the entire body) and *patka* (headgear). Some of them carry a *satka* additionally in their hand. The famous Gurugita asks the devotees not to copy the look or the behaviour of the Master. And it is accepted rule of law, in the master-disciple relationship in the spiritual world. Even the famous Shri Vivekananda never imitated the attire of his Guru, Sri Ramakrishna Paramhansa. Although some Sai devotees tend to dress like Baba out of ignorance and simply as a feel good factor, there are other fraudulent ones who try to impress the gullible devotees in order to extract money and other advantages. Some of these characters having copied the Masters dress style, go a further step. They try to copy the sitting postures of the Master (right leg over the left leg), and start speaking and blessing the other devotees, assuming to themselves the role of the Master himself. Some of them also prefix or suffix the word Sai to their names and bask in the glory of the name of Shri Sai. The temple pundits carrying on the daily worship usually wear a common dress code. However the devotees need not wear such dresses. They can wear any cloth that they usually wear when they are moving in a civilized society outside their homes. It is therefore the duty of the temple management to surely but politely impress upon such visitors to the temple to be properly attired and behave when they are in the temple premises.

On the day of Maha Samadhi of Baba, I invoke Shri Sai Baba's blessing for the devotees and readers in helping them to evolve in the spiritual path.

Guru Purnima Message 2007

Devotees are often heard to be grudging that Shri Sainath Maharaj or Baba is either angry with them or is not taking care of them as He used to before for reasons which they fail to comprehend or appreciate. Such an attitude indicates a highly personalized approach towards the Master. It is a unique feature of the Sai faith that the devotees get the personality and form of Baba even though His physical form is no more there. Psychologically they depend a lot on Shri Shirdi Sai for solace, guidance and more importantly for getting a solution to their day to day mundane problems. For most of the devotees He is a part of their lives. They worship Him, they read about Him, they meditate on Him, they do His Naamjaap, they talk about Him a lot without getting tired, hold Langers in His temples and donate alms to beggars in his name. Some of the ardent devotees even before taking any food or drink offer it to Baba mentally. Like children they collect all sorts of photographs, trinkets and other articles related to Baba and show these to other devotees as their proud possession. Such activities are a pointer to the fact that they are ever in search of Baba in their mind and soul and wish to establish an intense relationship with the Master.

It has been observed that when a devotee at first enters into the fold of Shri Sai Baba's divine and magnanimous personality, gets attracted to him in a very short time in a manner that our ordinary human reasoning cannot explain. When Baba was there in Shirdi many of the devotees used to go into a state of spiritual trance or sort of emotional hype at the very look of Baba. Such examples find a depiction in Shri Sai Satcharitra and many other books like Khaparde's diary etc. Such was the attraction of the master that when a non believer like Balasaheb Bhate met Baba for the first time, he looked at Him and just decided to stay back and settle down in Shirdi forever. Later he resigned from the government service only to serve Baba for the rest of his life. Having renounced the world he served Baba till the last day of his life and passed away at Shirdi.

Most of the devotees hold Baba's relation with them as their most prized possession. Before departing from his physical embodiment Baba had assured his devotees that he would continue to protect them from his invisible abode. He had even said that whenever His devotees would call him earnestly he would make his presence felt in some way or the other and also render help to remove their difficulties. Incidents happening in the lives of most of the devotees after Baba had taken Samadhi shows that Baba continues to keep his promise and help His devotees continuous till today.

Thus Shri Sainath Maharaj continues to render love, assurance and protection to all His devotees. At times being busy tackling their earthly problems, the devotees are not in a position to remember Baba as much as they used to do in earlier times. In such a situation, they start feeling an emotional vacuum in their hearts. Lets just compare this sense of void created in the devotee when the feeling towards the Sadguru reduces in its intensity with the example of the sun and sunlight. Rays of light continuously emanates from the sun and the sunlight falls on earth. When the sky is clouded the Sun's rays cannot be seen but nevertheless, the electromagnetic waves do fall on earth having penetrated the cloud. Similarly, Baba's love and protection towards the devotees flows continuously but some of the devotees do not experience it when their mind is engulfed with the worldly clouds.

Sai Nath Maharaj often used to tell devotees at Shirdi in no uncertain terms that whosoever offers prayers to him with intense faith would certainly receive His grace, help and certain experience relating to Him. Once the emotional rapport between the Guru and the pupil is established then the pupil is bound to go through a series of different emotional experiences. Sometimes he will feel flooded with loving emotions towards his master and sometimes he will feel a sense of emotional void. This bipolar emotional oscillation is not due to the fact that the Masters changing mood affects the pupil as perceived by devotees because a Perfect Master is a perfect soul. The reason for such a feeling in the devotee lies in the devotee himself. Hence, whenever such a situation arises the devotee should not get bogged down under his own emotional pressures and feel frustrated. Instead he should pray Baba to stabilize his emotional faith towards Him. Every devotee should try to understand that a Perfect Master has a thousand things to do for benefit of innumerable number of devotees staying at different places at the same time. Therefore to expect that the emotional needs of each devotee would be immediately fulfilled by the Guru is not the correct approach. Such an illogical mental state of the devotee only indicates a lack of faith in the Guru. If the devotee is convinced that the Sadguru is always busy in helping a large number of His devotees, at the same time, he (the devotee) should take care to see that he does not disturb the Master on his personal and frivolous issues. The best help a pupil can render to the Master is to leave Him to carry on His magnificent and universal work. This understanding on the part of the devotee will make the master comfortable.

Ram Navami Message 2007

OM SAI
"The Friend and Foe Syndrome/
Karma Siddhanta of the Hindus

When in distress we look around for someone to help us. We pray God for quick divine intervention to end our problem. We try to cash on the social position of our relatives and friends alike for this purpose. However, at times, get the desired help, all our efforts notwithstanding. On the other hand, at times, someone unexpectedly appears on the scene of our life and helps us out of the problem. Then when such an unexpected help arrives, we thank God for sending such a helpful friend. Thereafter while introducing this friend to others we address him as "my friend". In this context let us view the basic principles of 'karma theory' of the Hindu as propounded in our scriptures and practiced by the Spiritual Masters. A moot question need to be answered i.e. does or does not the cause and effect dynamics operate universally? The 'karma theory' would say that this helpful friend was an associated character of a certain past life and was to pay back the good act of rendering help which is known as Rinanubandh (payment of the past lives debts). It means that by one's good deeds of the past life (lives), one has earned this good and helpful friend. Be as it may, let us also examine the issue from the point of view of the sudden appearance of an enemy at a certain distressful point of time in life. When such a character suddenly appears then our immediate reaction begins from annoyance and leads up to revenge through anger. There after we normally start vilifying him and address him as "my enemy". That is how in our entire life we see our life full of "my friends" and "my enemies". But if "our friends" were created by our past deeds, which we glorify secretly then is it not logical that "our enemies" must also have been created by certain inimical acts committed by us in the past life (lives). Let us therefore agree to say that in our lives "my friends" and "my enemies" have to be dealt with equally, as both have been created by me and are "mine". Since both of them have been created due to karmic bandhan (Rinanubandh) of the past lives, isn't it our duty to neutralize the effects of both in this life so that we don't carry forward the seeds of cause-effect to the next life. Herein karma theory would say that a friend returns the pleasurable experience as we had given same or similar pleasurable experiences to him in a certain past life. Similarly an enemy would pay back the unpleasant or painful experience(s) because we had given him same or similar painful experience(s) to him in the past. When facing a situation of unhappiness created by the enemy we have two options to deal with him i.e. either by going through painful experience(s) neutralize its effects or by reacting adversely to carry forward the chain of reactions to the future lives.

Here comes-in the wisdom of saints like Shri Shirdi Sai Baba. The story of the frog and snake named as Chenbassapa and Veerbhadrappa respectively as illustrated in Shri Sai Satcharitra Chapter 47 is a pointer towards the correct answer to our question. As the story goes, Baba once heard the painful sound of a frog, when he was moving in a village. Being moved by the painful sound He searched for the frog and found him on the river shore and saw that a snake was trying to swallow it. On seeing the snake and the frog in the situation of deadly animosity, He tried to separate them by reminding them of their inimical relationship in a past life. Baba told the snake i.e. Veerbhadrappa, that he and the frog Bassappa had killed each other in the past life as the result of a bitter rivalry. He advised the snake to let go of the frog, listening to what Baba said, Veerbhadrappa (the snake) released the frog (Bassappa) who jumped to the river and escaped. Shri Sai Baba has advised His devotees not to react sharply and adversely towards enemies with equal and opposite negativities but to allow negative effects of past karmas reflected through the enemy to neutralize gradually.

This highly evolved and critical theory of Karma (cause and effects) can perhaps be better understood through a simple example. Suppose one releases an arrow from a bow, then what happens! The arrow at the release point will move with the highest velocity and will gradually slow down due to mid-air friction and take a curvaceous path due to the gravity of earth before hitting the target. However, the moment it hits the target or failing which hits the earth, its force gets neutralized. This means that more the distance the arrow travels lesser the less momentum it creates at the impact point. Greater distance means greater time and less impact. When we assimilate the basic principles of these two theories of metaphysics and physics, we come to the conclusion that instead of directly reacting to an enemies' wrath, it is wiser to show a little tolerance and allow time to reduce the impact of the inimical act of the enemy. When Shri Sai Baba spoke of "Saburi" it included this aspect of handling of enemies with patience and consideration. This message of the seers which have been handed over to the human society from time to time is unfortunately lost sight of and this is the cause of most of the social malice that we face today.

Let us pray Shri Sai to give us the intellect and wisdom to make tomorrow's world a happier place to stay by following his principle of "Shraddha" and "Saburi".

New Year Message 2007

Most of the devotees of Shri Shirdi Sai Baba are reported to have been receiving spiritual experiences, many of which are in the form of miracles. Such thoughts of actual or perceived miracles not only enhances their faith in Baba but also spiritually uplifts them. If one goes through such similar experiences of the devotees as depicted in Shri Sai Satcharitra and other literature on Sai Baba and compares them with the experiences of the present day devotees one would find a close similarity between them. Shri Khaparde, a prominent advocate of Amravati near Nagpur, who used to visit Shirdi frequently, and Kakasaheb Dixit who devoted the later part of his life in the services of Baba at Shirdi have recorded details of such experiences in their diaries, they use to maintain.

When one hears about some of the common experiences reported by devotees, one's mind is transported to the time of Baba at Shirdi. Imaginations become vivid, all worries cease to exist and time seems to stand still. Most devotees have reported that they used to get spiritually charged at the very sight of Baba; disturbing and uncontrollable thoughts of their mind used to vanish, and a feeling of purity and love engulfs them.

Baba had a unique way of communicating with his devotees through language, look and touch besides the extremely strong and vibrant spiritual thought waves He used to send. He used to send His thought waves even from afar. These powerful thought waves used to appear in the form of vivid dreams and ideas in the minds of His devotees and used to convey certain impulses, directions, forewarnings, future happenings and love waves of Baba. Those who followed these directions with an open mind benefited amply. When such directions were related by Baba in dreams, the results were seen taking shape suddenly or in due course of time in the actual realities of their worldly life. For example, one devotee saw Baba giving him yellow rice particles in his dream. When he got up he found yellow rice sprinkled all over his bed. Similarly another devotee found a coconut in his bed when awakened from sleep having seen Baba. Another direct experience as depicted in the Shri Sai Satcharitra Chapter 40 was in 1917, when Hemadpant had a dream wherein he saw Baba in the form of a Sanyasi promising to come to take meal at Hemadpant's house on that day. At lunchtime, just as the family was about to begin eating, two men, Ali Mahomed and Moulana Ismu Mujavar, appeared at the door and handed over a picture of Sai Baba to Hemadpant. Hemadpant was much moved at the thought that Baba as promised had indeed blessed him by gracing his house for lunch in the form of a painting.

There are numerous experiences about Baba appearing in a physical form in different and distant places, while he was actually in his human form at Shirdi. Devotees have reported that Baba, while sitting in front of the Dhuni in the morning at the mosque, would often refer to His visit to distant places and other worlds he had visited overnight despite being physically present at Shirdi. A famous incident that took place in 1910 is narrated in Shri Sai Satcharitra Chapter 7, when Baba, sitting near the Dhuni (fire) and was pushing firewood into it. Suddenly He pushed his arm into the Dhuni as a result of which His hand got burnt. Some devotees who were sitting near Him forcibly pulled His hand out of fire. On enquiry by the shocked devotees, He replied that in a village a little away from Shirdi, the wife of a blacksmith was working in the furnace with her child tied to her waist. When her husband called her, she suddenly got up and the child slipped into the furnace. As a spontaneous reaction Baba thrust his hand into the Dhuni to save the child from the furnace. Later the couple visited Shirdi with the child and thanked Him for having saved the child. Another devotee, B.V Deo had sent a letter to Bapu Saheb Jog in Shirdi requesting Baba's presence in a group lunch he had arranged. Baba promised to attend the lunch with two other persons and did so by appearing in the form of a Sanyasi with two followers.

The greater miracles of Baba show instances of control of natural forces like fire, air and water (rain). The Satcharitra chapter 11 narrates about an evening when torrential rain accompanied by lightning and thunderstorm hit Shirdi flooding it entirely. This terrified all the people of Shirdi, devotees, animals and birds who took refuge at Dwarakamayee Masjid and prayed Baba for help. At their request Baba commanded the cloud in a thunderous voice to stop its fury and to allow his children to go their houses. Within minutes the rain stopped and the storm settled down. Another instance documented in Shri Sai Satcharitra chapter 11 was about an incident when flames from Baba's dhuni rose up to the roof of Dwarakamai Masjid threatening to burn it. Baba took his satka (stick) and started hitting a pillar commanding the fire to calm down. At each stroke of the satka the flames gradually started coming down. Soon the situation normalized. Baba gave numerous other types of experiences to his devotees but it would not be possible to codify or cite such examples due to lack of space. The more surprising and interesting fact to note is that even after departure from His bodily abode in 1918 and till the present day, devotees continue to report similar experiences relating to Baba some of which are in the nature of miracles . Truly speaking, even on the day Baba left his body and thereafter, devotees have been experiencing such unexplainable events. Such experiences of Baba are not limited to the gullible and uneducated rural folks of India as is commonly believed to be, but cuts across the "intelligentsia" of the society including lawyers, professors, officials, doctors, scientists and others. It is interesting to observe that even in this era of science and technology dominated individualism, with population (the number of devotees) having increased manifold, where rationality and objectivity rules the minds of the people, such spiritual experiences at times bordering on miracles continue to affect millions. Cutting across the man made differentiations of race, religion, caste, socio-economic diversities etc., all are making a beeline to Baba's Samadhi at Shirdi as Baba had once uttered in a state of spiritual ecstasy. Despite the modern day youth's affinity with the western culture, Baba's message remains ever relevant and appealing. Today's modern youth and children with all their scientific temperament are staunch believers of Baba and find Him to be the solution to all their problems. That is why so many temples have come up across the globe. Sai Baba not only crossed the boundaries of humanism but gave shelter to all living creatures. The Sai Satcharitra narrates numerous instances of His acts of compassion towards dogs, snakes, horses, tigers and even birds.

Today on an average 35,000 to 40,000 people visit Shirdi every day and on weekends the numbers go upto lakhs. The phenomenal growth in the Sai movement as can be seen in the astronomical growth in the number of temples, literary publications, devotional music CDs and numerous T.V. coverages etc. The number of devotees dedicated to spread the name and message of Shri Shirdi Sai Baba is mind-boggling. Today the Sai movement is not limited only to Maharashtra as was the situation during the time of Baba. Within decades of His departure it has crossed the national boundaries to become a global movement. This new era of "Saiism" does not only touch on the religious aspect of the devotee's life only but affects and permeates all other aspects of a devotees life (family, culture, social behavior etc). For the devotees, Shri Sai Baba is not a part of their life but their life itself in all its aspects.

The spirit of Sai is more active and alive today than what it ever was. This raises a fundamental question - "Who is Sai Baba?" Some address him as a Sadguru, some as a fakir, some as a Yogiraj, some as a saint and most of the devotees Him as "God the Almighty" Himself. He has been accepted as an incarnation (Saguna Sakara Avatara), which means, God who walked on the earth in human form. History has shown that the expansion of religions and faiths started by the incarnations expands phenomenally after they left their human embodiment. This was the case with Jesus Christ, Buddha, Mohammed and Shri Krishna. The Sai movement is on the increase exponentially in a similar manner, which goes to reinforce the faith that Sai Baba was an incarnation of God (Paramatma). It further goes to prove one of the promises of Baba that after leaving his body he will be ever active from his tomb to protect and guide his devotees. As Baba had once promised, He continues to exist in a subtle form (Mahakarana sheath) as a unifying force, to spread and re-establish compassion, love, truth and tolerance amongst human beings and among all living entities on earth.

Let us welcome and embrace this age of Sai, who is the panacea for all the evils of the present world, torn asunder by forces of regionalism, racialism, economic and social differences, religious bigotry, fanaticism and lack of faith in "God". Let us look forward to a happier tomorrow; let the name of Shri Sai resonate in all corners of the globe.

Dussehra Message 2006

When Shri Sai Baba of Shirdi was in His human embodiment at Shirdi, thousands of people of different regions, religions, languages and categories used to visit Him. The young and the old, married and unmarried, worldly people and spiritual seekers and many others representing the cross-section of the society used to approach the Master, to get his help and blessings to satisfy their material needs and spiritual aspirations. In Shri Sai Satcharitra, one finds mention about these characters although there were many more about whom there is no record.

Sadgurus like Shri Shirdi Sai Baba, operate simultaneously at two levels of consciousness. Some of their activities are visible and some are non- visible in nature. Examples of some of the manifested activities are like feeding the poor and the devotees, curing physical and mental diseases, rendering temporal assistance in material needs and religious pursuits of the devotees etc. The manner in which He used to give relief was miraculous at times. Hundreds of families of Shirdi and outside used to depend on Him for relief and sustenance in their worldly existence. Sai Baba never refused to help any one who approached Him. He laboured day in and day out to solve the complex problems of His devotees even when He was in an indifferent health. Once He told a devotee that He (Baba) could not sleep during the previous night thinking about that devotee. "What would happen to my people, if I constantly do not keep an eye on them" He used to say. This was the role of a Provider and a Protector.

However, the other role of Shri Sai Baba was subtle and secretive in nature, which added permanent value to the lives of the people that approached Him. Shri Shirdi Sai Baba was a Perfect Master or a Sadguru. Being a Sadguru His divine charter of duties was to train the devotees with a view to evolve their mental and emotional qualities and ultimately to lead them towards emancipation. Such a process of evolution, when left to the disciple himself, is very slow and may take a number of lives to achieve. As ordained by the law of nature, every human being evolves during each life cycle while on the earth plane by experiencing an un-calculable number of events that generate pleasure or pain. Without, the help of a Master or Sadguru who has traveled along and experienced the path of spiritual evolution, the seeker has to go through an audacious process of trials and errors and in the way his evolution slows down. However, if one accepts a Sadguru as his mentor, and strictly abides by His advice, his evolution becomes easier and faster. The Sadguru with His divine powers and qualities has immense capabilities to hasten the process of evolution of all beings that come in contact with Him. Therefore, He is called a Samarth (capable of giving God realisation) Sadguru. However, notwithstanding the ceaseless effort of the Masters all devotees do not progress spiritually at an equal pace. The pace of evolution of a devotee depends on a few Prime factors, like, acceptance of the Master-both intellectually and emotionally, as the sole guide and Protector in the spiritual journey, complete faith in and adherence to the advice and commands of the Master and finally a lot of patience under all trying circumstances and stretched over long periods of time to follow the Master's prescriptions in its true spirit. (Quote from Shri Sai Satcharitra Chapter 18 & 19)

Usually the Perfect Masters like Baba do not force disciples to follow their advice. They suggest the prescriptions directly (through words, actions and direct experiences etc.) and/or indirectly (through dreams, anecdotes, hints and mediums etc.) to each disciple or some times to a group of disciples. Baba at times used to speak cryptic or broken sentences or utter a certain un-intelligible language. The devotees could comprehend its meaning only after a protracted mental deliberation or discussion with others over the issue. Baba can always give a direct solution to all the problems but His method has been to lead the devotee through a self-finding and analytical mental process. Many a times He would enquire from some devotees as to what they were talking about when they were together. He would then advise them on how to handle the compulsive and negative thoughts of mind and to inculcate a habit of generating positive thoughts. The omniscient Sadguru used to keep a watch on the negative and positive thoughts of His disciples and numerous such examples can be found in Shri Sai Satcharitra. Baba used to create thought waves in the minds of devotees by His subtle powers thereby leading them to find a solution to their own problems. To many, He used to give directions in dreams as well. He used to render such help with a view to create a clearer and purer state of mind in the devotees, which is essentially required to progress in the path of spiritual evolution. The Sadgurus do not believe in keeping their disciples dependent on Them for all times to come with a view to get continued personal service from them. They only desire is to evolve the disciples to the state of a perfect human being (Satpurush), with perfect noble qualities so that these evolved souls can further carry on certain subtle and difficult tasks on this earth or elsewhere in accordance with the Divine Plan. The Sadgurus not only gives emancipation to the human-souls under their care but they also create a few spiritual workers from among the evolved devotees to assist them in their universal and subtle activities. The basic principle they follow is to light a number of candles from a single candle and they expect the process to continue generation wise for all times to come. This is known as the 'Guru Marg' or the "Path of the Teachers"

If we analyse the various methods that Shri Sai adopted while dealing with different devotees, one of His objectives stands out prominently i.e. the qualitative evolution of mind of the disciples. In whatever He did towards the training of His devotees, the moot idea of Baba was to evolve not only the mental qualities but also the thought process itself. For example, when Nana Saheb Chandorkar sitting near Baba at Dwarakamayee Masjid was attracted by the beauty of a woman, Baba never advised him not to look at women. (Quote from Shri Sai Satcharitra Chapter 49) What He advised was that while looking at any beautiful woman or beautiful object, one should think of 'beauty' as an aspect of God's creation. He further emphasized on the internal beauty of the soul and not on the external beauty of the body. The lesson that Baba gave was that when the mind is attracted to anything, it is better to attach a higher value to the thought itself rather than to struggle with mind to avoid the object of attraction.

No one can struggle with his own mind, as it is the most powerful force in human beings as ordained by nature. The moment one tries to struggle with mind in order to erase an evil thought or enforce a good thought sheerly by one's will, it is bound to create certain reactions and such reactions is likely to lead to further problems. This is the most difficult task for any human being to perform, living as he does in a complex world. Therefore, Baba used to keep a constant watch on the thoughts arising in the minds of His devotees and guide them promptly.

For example Baba had through Mhalsapati asked Kaka Saheb Dixit to stay quietly (Uge-muge) in Dixit-Wada at Shirdi and not to mix with others. He told Dixit that he should be wary of thieves in the Wada lest they would take away everything, meaning thereby loss of positive quality of his mind and peace. Similarly Upasani Baba was asked to stay at Khandoba temple and not to meet any one. He was not even allowed to meet Baba who was sitting a few hundred yards away at Dwarakamayee masjid for a long time. By separating the genuine seekers from the rest of the world, Baba wanted them to maintain a purer and positive state of mind and not to get contaminated by the negative thoughts of others as usually happens in social interactions. Baba used to render advice in the same or similar line to different devotees e. g. to keep one's promise always, to make adequate payment for the services received from any person, to tolerate and not to quarrel even if provoked, to avoid speaking ill of others, to avoid differentiating between human beings on the grounds of material or social differentiation etc. and finally to visualise the presence of God in every living being, object, every thought and every feeling.

All religious rituals including Poojas, Aartis and Parayanas, etc. are methods of the human mind evolution at the first stage. Evolution of the thought process of mind in itself is the inter-mediary stage and emancipation of the soul through realization of God is the third and final stage in the spiritual journey of the soul. Since the omniscient Baba could easily read through the thoughts of all His devotees, He could prescribe specific methods of thought control and spiritual evolution to each of His devotees.

History shows that it is the positive forces of human mind that had built mighty civilizations and it is the negative forces of human minds that had brought about the total destruction of their own civilizations as seen in the case of the Romanian, Egyptian and Peru civilization etc. We see the world as our mind visualises it and our visualisation is limited and often distorted. We see the world with a fixed Kaleidoscope from a certain angle. If the Kaleidoscope is rotated, then different forms and patterns of life would appear. Since each individual sees life from a certain fixed angle, each experiences a specific pattern, and this pattern of life experienced by him seems to be the only truth. Let alone the people with a predominantly evil nature, even people with the best of qualities suffer from this limitation of mental fixity. It is seen that at times the best quality of an individual, become the greatest block in his evolution in certain situations. For example, there was a kind person who used to help every one. He had the expectation, as is usually the case with human beings that others would be equally kind to him and reciprocate, in his bad days. But when he was in distress every one did not render the required help in the manner and to the extent he had rendered to them. As a result, he started questioning the very plinth of kindness and decided not to help others as he used to do earlier. Now his proactive kindness turned to reactive narrow-mindedness. His evolved quality of natural benevolence was blocked and the evolution process of mind slowed down. No doubt as a worldly-wise person he went a step forward but in his spiritual evolution he had gone a step backward. If he had the flexibility of mind to accept that imperfection is bound to exist in others without passing value judgment over the imperfect conduct of others, he would have been happier and more evolved. The lesson to learn is that howsoever perfect one claims to be, the universal nature (containing both so called perfect and imperfect aspects), does not give a license to any one condemn others, howsoever, imperfect. Therefore, our Seers have proclaimed that one may hate sin but not the sinner. Baba unequivocally declared that when any one condemned any one else, his feelings were hurt.

Some psycho-analysts hold the view that perfectionists suffer psychological stress the most as they find it difficult to adjust with the imperfect circumstances or the imperfect traits in the character of others with whom they interact. Such persons are sometimes, highly creative because of their sense of perfection but nevertheless they suffer the most due to a psychologically social maladjustment. This problem of human beings is not limited to a category alone. It is more or less with every one to some extent. The fundamental problem with the magnificent human being is that each human being considers himself to be the centre of the Universe – the little Universe he has created for himself. Therefore, he desires that every thing around him should fall in line with his requirements of that little Universe. They are not prepared to visualise themselves as an infinitesimally small particle in the vast Universe with millions and millions of ever changing patterns. These millions of little Universes of human ego juxtaposed in the social fabric of our complex world try to clash with each other and to pull each other apart by the gravitational force of their individualism or ego. The Sadgurus have always tried to give simple solutions to this complex problem of human society.

If we follow the prescriptions of Baba, as contained in Shri Sai Satcharitra our thought process can go through a qualitative change and we can have a clearer picture of the world around and our reliance in the vast universe. It will not only do good to us but also to others around us. Therefore, when reading Shri Sai Satcharitra or other literature on Baba, our thought should always be focused on the aspect of conscious mental evolution that Baba repeatedly taught and exemplified through his own conduct.

Guru Purnima Message 2006

Ever since the phenomenon of Shri Shirdi Sai extensively caught public attention in India and outside, there has been a relentless stream of speculation as well as concerted effort on the question of His parentage i.e. whether he was born a Hindu or a Muslim. The result of such research by different researchers has turned out to be either speculative or controversial since it is based more on circumstantial evidence as opposed to primary data. However, my efforts are channelised into finding out who and what Baba is rather than what was His parentage or where he was born.

There can be no denial in any quarter that Shri Shirdi Sai Baba is a divine personality of the highest order who demonstrated magnificent qualities of selfless service to all, who came in contact with Him, without least consideration of His self. He was not constrained by the limitations of any organized religion or path as is amply evidenced by His acceptance of disciples from all religions, cultures, castes and paths etc. There was no question of economic and social differentiation in His scheme of things. Besides non-possession and non-attachment, he was divinely magnanimous and empathetic towards the poorest of the poor among His devotees, as well as animals and birds. He also possessed wonderful powers of miracles, which he often used to help His disciples in distress, even from a distance.

Given this universal theme of His approach, one can safely conclude that Shri Sai Baba demonstrated the highest qualities of Hindu philosophy in His actual life, notwithstanding whether He was born of Hindu or Muslim parentage.

When one speaks of Hinduism at first one has to understand as to what Hinduism stands for in its essence. Some historians comment that the word 'Hindu' was originally 'Indu' coming out of 'Indus valley civilization' but some foreigners called it Hindu like 'Hindukush' mountain. Hinduism in its quintessence is rather a way of life than merely being a Hindu path of worship of deities. It prescribes numerous paths to its people and leaves them free to choose any one. It prescribes the worship of a number of divine forms (Devatas/Devis) and also the worship of the formless (Brahman – the ultimate God).

Hinduism does not insist or force conversion of people to its Hindu fold and failing which their extinction. It has never believed in religious expansionism with the help of sword and always believed in the peaceful co-existence of all religions. This highest level of tolerance of the Hindus has led to the absorption of many conquering or colonizing races, following different paths, into its all embracing fold. Sufism, which truly believes in the unity of souls and tolerance among people following different paths, therefore, found a strong base in India – the soil of Hindus.

Basically what Shri Shirdi Sai Baba practiced and taught is spiritualism and humanism as against bigotry, obscurantism, blind faith and intolerance. To that extent He was a genuine Hindu and a genuine Sufi amalgamated in a single human form. He often used to say 'Allah Malik hai' or 'Ishwar Achha karega' or 'Sabka Malik ek hai' i.e., the one and ultimate God called Ishwar or Allah is the sovereign power who controls everyone and everything. This is the monistic "Advaitya" philosophy of the Hindus. On the other hand, He never deterred His Hindu devotees from going to any temples to worship any deity of their faith. Similarly he never stopped the Muslims from taking out the Tazia procession or doing anything prescribed by their religion at Shirdi etc. Indeed He encouraged both and ensured, at Shirdi, tolerance towards the religious sentiments of devotees practicing various faiths, through mutual participation in each others festivals. Not only for the residents of Shirdi but also for the outsiders who used to visit Him in great numbers, He was not only a Guru but a part of their entire existence. Shri Sai had permeated into all aspects of the lives of His devotees – religion, family, festivals, way of earning and spending, social conduct, moral conduct, cultural activities, births and deaths, diseases and cures and even regarding the rearing of children and pets. Baba's influence has been so strong and wide that even two to three generations of family members would come together to seek His blessings and advice on various matters at Shirdi. Every one looked up to Him as a God in human form and also as the head of the family and surrendered to Him. The way of life not only for the natives of Shirdi, but those visiting Baba, metamorphosized to a new way of looking at life which Baba taught them through His conduct and precepts. Thus, like Hinduism, the path shown by Shri Sai has become a way of life for His devotees rather than a religious and ritualistic path alone. Even today the same Sai spirit pervades the lives of millions. It is because of this universality and simplicity, He is accepted by all and He is being worshipped.

This is what explains the unimaginable expansion of the Sai path not only in India, but in other countries. Shri Sai remains, as promised by Him, a living Master, with His all-pervasive spirit that controls the entire life of His devotees. Such a magnificent, universal and time-less divine personality is termed as "Vasudeva" in Hinduism. And the spirit of Shri Vasudeva is eternal.

Ram Navami Message 2006

The path towards the Sadguru is the real and easiest path, more so in this age of confusion, conflicts, and cruel materialism. As Swami Vivekananda had said like all rivers leading to the sea, all the paths that men take lead to Him, the God eternal. The paths that are mostly adopted by the seekers are Rajyoga, Gyanayoga, Karmayoga, Bhaktiyoga, Hathayoga, Layayoga, Nivriti Marg, Pravriti Marg etc. There also are Avadhootas, Kapalikas, Aghoris and many other types of seekers. Various religions have different approaches towards spiritualism and religion. In this multiplicity of approaches towards God realization, there has to be something common and universal that must be all pervading. For seekers of this universal path it is easier to make spiritual progress with comparative ease.

Sitting in the dilapidated Masjid at Shirdi, Baba once said that there are many paths to God, but one of the paths leading to God is through the Dwarkamayee (i.e. the Masjid where He used to live). When one analyses how Baba led thousands of people towards God realization at Shirdi a certain pattern is discernable. The basic principles of the Sai path are based on the existence in physical form of a perfect being known variously as a Perfect Master, a Sadguru, or a Qutub as called by the Sufis. A Qutub simply means an axis, a pivot around which the living and non-living existence of this world revolves. The Perfect Master, having gone through the experiences of the different stages of evolution including that of a man at last reaches the stage of God. However, those among these perfect divine beings, who, out of infinite compassion, make the greatest sacrifice of not enjoying the blissful state of God but incarnate on earth in a human body to serve the imperfect, suffering humanity, are called the perfect Masters. As Meher Baba has said, at any point of time there are five

Perfect Masters on earth in an embodied form. In my view they are possibly more in number

When in a human body, they simultaneously live the lives of the human beings and Gods. In the state of God, they have infinite power, infinite knowledge, infinite happiness and infinite existence. Like God they are Omnipotent, Omnipresent and Omniscient and enjoy the powers of controlling nature. They share their power, knowledge and pleasure with millions of human beings by certain methods both perceivable and unperceivable by human beings. Such acts of the Avataras or Masters and are known as Leelas or divine miracles. All miracles are based on the laws of nature. Only one has to know experience and master them. All the elemental and subtle forces of nature like fire, water, air etc., on earth defined as deities by the Hindus work under their command or wish of these Masters when they are carrying on their divine functions. As Gods they see everything in themselves and themselves in everything. So they serve everyone without any differentiation as if they are serving themselves. They see God in everyone even though others may not be able to see the God in them. They give infinite love compassion and help to others and take on themselves infinite pain for others. Once any human being or a member of any other species is linked with them in any manner, they ensure that the jiva is gradually evolved, life after life, till it merges with God from where it came. This ultimate stage of evolution is ordinarily known as Mukti or Moksha.

These Perfect Masters alone are capable of leading human being to God realization. They follow what is common and universal in all religions i.e. humanism based on love. Out of love they not only take care of the spiritual evolution of the devotees but also their temporal requirements. Once one has surrendered to them they look after all his needs as a mother would do for an infant. They can go to any extent, even to sacrifice their human body; to protect their children. That's what Baba used to do for His devotees as can be read in Shri Sai SatCharitra and as is being experienced by many even today. To develop closer and closer links with a Sadguru like Baba, one has to patiently develop faith in Him even under the most trying circumstances. The devotee has also to develop the qualities of humility, sacrifice, tolerance and steadfastness in devotion and all his actions as desired by the Sadguru. Baba used to give visions to many people in the form of their deities like Hanuman, Ganesh etc., which convinced them that there was no difference between Baba and any other deity or even God. One can therefore, at the first stage, try to experience the forms of other deities in Baba, and worship Him in the method in which these deities are worshipped. In short, one should try to see everything in and seek everything from Baba. This path may be difficult at the initial stage but can certainly be achieved with steadfastness and faith in Baba. I have no doubts in my mind that a devotee concentrating his entire spiritual thought and energy on Baba will progress faster towards spiritual evolution than by following other ways of worship. In any case in any or all systems of worship the Guru becomes the Prime factor to motivate and lead the disciple towards enlightenment and emancipation.

New Year Message 2006

Shirdi Sai Baba of Shirdi has become a phenomena of today.

This can safely be stated on the basis of the unexpected and innumerable gamut of activities taking place in India and the world towards the propagation of the path and preachings of the Sai baba of Shirdi. It is seen that in the last few years the Shirdi Sai Sansthan at Shirdi has expanded its activities multi-fold to cope with the ever increasing number of visitors to Shirdi. This rate of expansion is very much expected given the fact that an average of about 40 to 50 thousand devotees visit Shirdi daily. On important days it goes up to a few lakhs. What is amaz-ing is the construction and opening of hundreds and hun-dreds of Shirdi Sai Baba temples and other related institu-tions in India and abroad through the self-motivation of the devotees. Shirdi Sai Baba had never setup any institutions. Would one historically examine the way in which temples have been created by devotees following other paths, it would became clear that usually the main trust opens its branches at other places as the first step. Then the main trust and the branches take up temple construction projects which in-cludes planning, financing, constructing and supervising etc. But in name of Shri Sainath Maharaj, self-motivated devotees and groups are themselves creating re-sources, constructing temples and carrying out a num-ber of other religious and charitable activities without any main organizations controlling these. No doubt such self-motivation is a result of the existing spirit of Shri Sai.

Most devotees of Baba are emotively linked with Him and are prepared to undergo any amount of hardship and sacrifice to do a task in His name. The rate at which the number of His devotees and institu-tions are multiplying is simply astounding. There are a large number of publications about Baba in various languages in the form of books, journals, magazines, book-lets running to thousands. Devotees are ever avid to know more and more details about Baba when He was at Shirdi as also the happenings of today relating to Him. There are a large number of web-sites on Baba in the internet, created in India and abroad.

Notwithstanding these multi faced activities, one important aspect which is seriously required to spread the name of Shri Sai Baba is prominently lacking. That is, serious research on Baba, using the modem research methodol-ogy is much below the desired standards. Some scholars from India and abroad, independently or through research institutions, have made substantial contribution in research and some books and research findings in the form of articles have been published. However, a study of these volumes would indicate that the researchers/authors have not had access to many of the important documents pub-lished during Baba's time and there-after. This is because initially most of the books and articles written on Baba were in Marathi language and later English versions or original writings in English came to market. There is hardly any library that has a comprehensive collection of literature on Baba.

To undertake serious research, a good library maintain-ing the required documents like books, journals, newspaper items, manuscripts hand-written notings, photo-graphs, paintings, sketches, maps, research papers and well maintained bibliography is a must. Unfortunately no such library is in existence, to enable the researches on Baba to undertake serious study. Some devotees, particularly the writers, are in possession of some of the important docu-ments but what is needed is to create a single forum/ body that possesses and maintains this for posterity. It should be the endeavor of each devotee to collect all such records of the past and maintain them properly for use by future researchers. That would be a great contribution for Baba's cause. Let us resolve to work towards this end in the New Year to come.

Dussehra Message 2005

There are a few major differences between other species and the human beings. Human beings or the homo-sapiens race has established itself as the most superior race on this earth because of the superiority of its mental faculties. These capacities grew stage by stage through innumerable stages of evolution of nature on itself. What we call as nature is the limited manifestation of the sovereign divine power called Brahma or God. That ultimate power manifested as universe, solar systems and planets etc. Thereafter, it created the living organisms, birds, animals and ultimately human beings through different stages of growth in consciousness to habitat on our planet called earth.

All other species have instinctive intelligence but what human beings exclusively possess is intellect. This intellectual consciousness of a man is a combination of his mental faculties like memory, recall, analytical ability and also qualities of heart like love-hatred, selfishness-self sacrifice, anger-calmness, intolerance--patience etc. The highly developed human brain which is much greater than any computer, takes all these factors into consideration in giving a solution to any problem. It is again this intellect that has created the loftiest and greatest systems in the earth - social, economic, religious, political and spiritual etc.

Man's intellect has penetrated into the micro world of elements and the macro dimensions of space. During the last two to three decades we have witnessed what is termed as "intellectual explosion" in the world. Movements in the space, cloning of animals, transplantation of human organs, sub-earth discoveries, micro analysis of elements, wire-less communication, to mention a few, have revolutionalised human civilization and given human beings immense power to control the forces of nature, almost bordering on divinity.

Commensurately, the pressure on human brain has increased tremendously. Newer concepts are entering into our thinking system or thought process making the old concepts redundant. It is happening so fast that most of us are finding it difficult to adjust to this rapid transition whereas it is easy for the new generations to adjust at a faster pace due to the nascent state of their mind. The older generations find it to be heavily at odds with their old concepts and style of thinking. This obviously is creating a lot of mal-adjustment in individuals with different levels of sensitivities and also greater mal-adjustment in the social fabric. Such mal-adjustments are reflecting in the assertion of selfish individualism beyond proportions, discords between parents and off-springs, large number of divorce in marital life, material approach to emotional aspects of life and a mad race to compete in the material world with others at the cost of finer aspects of life. This happened in many civilizations earlier and by the law of self-contradiction these civilizations fell and lost their glory. Such a mal-adjustment between the material and the emotional world brought the downfall of the mighty Roman, Egyptian, Mexican, Persian and many other civilizations.

The answer to such confusion does not lie in the assertion of atomic egoism or selfish individualism at the cost of greater social good but to accept the ways of others, with their perfections and imperfections. Love is not acceptance of only the best in the loved one but is the total acceptance of the entire personality. This is what Baba preached and practiced at Shirdi. Only He was capable of bringing the divergent groups of individuals belonging to different castes, religions, creeds and different socio-economic status under a single banner - i.e. the banner of humanism at Shirdi. The world needs to follow this concept today, to make tomorrow a better place to live.

Guru Purnima Message 2005

Any attempt to understand and value the spiritual world on the basis of the purely materialistic knowledge of the mundane world is an exercise in futility. On the other hand, one who has tread along the spiritual path and has gained direct knowledge can handle the material world in a much better manner. Even if both spiritual and materialistic paths emanate from the same God, the spiritual path is finer and purer. It is not possible for any worldly man, to leave the material world and enter the spiritual world suddenly sheerly by his will and volition. Such a path is for the true spiritual practitioners, known as Yogis, Munis or Sanyasis. However, the spiritual depth and value of these true spiritual practitioners cannot be assessed by seeing the examples of frauds who can be found everywhere these days. Yet most of the gullible people get attracted to them because of their attractive attire and speech. Since most of the people live in the world of illusory greatness with a limited and distorted mind-set, they easily get attracted to such actors. However, human beings who are purer and simpler in nature instinctively do not get attracted towards them. Such people generally get attracted and attached when they come in contact with some purer souls like the genuine saints and Sadgurus. The impurer ones generally accept the impure human beings, projecting themselves as spiritual characters or Gurus. The purer souls accept only the true Saints as their Gurus. This obviously leads to the conclusion that one's Guru is what one wants and selects him to be. Or it may be said that the Guru is what one thinks him to be.

There are two types of people. Some of them are capable of seeing the positive side (Shubha) of every thing and there are others who are capable of seeing the negative side (Ashubha) of every thing. A man with an impure mental vision can cause much harm to himself as his mind gets contaminated with the negative traits of his own thoughts progressively. He ultimately becomes a prisoner of his own thought and sees the worst in everyone and everything around even when he is in a temple or in association with the other purer souls. As the worldly people going through the experience of negatives and positives in life try to evolve themselves out of their negativities so also the spiritually evolved souls (even with lots of positive qualities) continuously strive to eradicate their remaining negative qualities in them. Thus, all human beings the evil and good alike are at different stages of consciousness are in the continuous process of evolution.

The theories of different religions as also the different theories of Psychology agrees on one point that ultimately a man's nature gets conditioned by what he thinks continuously. One who continuously thinks about the bad qualities in others, ultimately develops those qualities in him. The same is true of continuous good thoughts. One finds an interesting story in "Shri Sai Satcharitra" about this. A person used to speak ill of another person at Shirdi when Shirdi Sai Baba was there. Later when he met Baba, He asked him to look at the pig devouring dirt with relish and commented – "look how happily he is eating the dirt. You have been speaking ill of your brother to your utter satisfaction and so your nature has become as evil."

Thus in this world of material illusions even educated people, coming in contact with people harbouring evil thoughts against others, get easily contaminated. Far to speak of spiritual evolution, such an approach towards others ultimate leads them morally downwards. The best way to save one from such a situation is to pray Baba when a negative thought comes to mind or to recite his name silently or read Shri Sai Satcharitra.

Ram Navami Message 2005

God is addressed differently by different groups of people and also personally by individuals through various names. God, the unseen, is thus addressed differently as He does not have a single form. His manifested forms are millions and millions. These forms maybe visible to the human eye or may not be. He has gross forms, subtle forms, energy forms, thought forms, feeling forms. But the ultimate form of God is an unseen form, which no one has seen. All Saints, paths and religions, at their best, have called it a vast, timeless, spaceless, causeless, attributeless ocean of emptiness or a primordial void

Whatever God reveals about Himself through the sense and beyond perceptions to the human beings, is what they understand Him to be. Species other than human beings are not mentally evolved to conceptualize that the movements in the universe and also in them are created by God as their soul-force. The excellence and superiority of the homo-sapiens lies here. Not only do they have the capacity to conceptualise God in myriads of forms but they have also worked through the methods to experience God at different stages of consciousness. Whereas other religions have conceptualized a limited number of these forms of God, Hinduism, being one of the oldest religions on this earth has created thousands of symbols for millions of aspects of the unlimited God. This has not happened in a day or year. It has evolved through the passage of time of thousands of years through the experience of practitioners who have devoted their full lives to the realm of spiritualism.

The universally accepted principle of experiencing God can be explained through the parallelism of a river meeting an ocean or sea. All rivers emanating from different places (locations), meandering through different lands and paths ultimately merge in sea. Thereafter, forever the river is a part of the sea. It merges its total identity in it. When we think of the Bay of Bengal, we do not picturise is it as a combination of the Ganges, Brahmaputra and other similar rivers and thousands of other water channels merging in it. Herein comes the concept of multiplism and dualism leading to Monism (Advaita). Since each of these rivers flows on different soils, through different hills and forests, takes different curves and falls, the attributes of the water it carries cannot be the same - i.e., in content, speed, density, quality and quantity. However, once merged in the sea, all its qualities merge and become one with the attributes of the seawater.

Different religions and paths that people follow are like these different rivers. It is wrong to criticize any of these religions and paths. One is free to practice any path he chooses, but is socially and morally not free to slander other religions or paths.

This is what Shri Sai Nath Maharaj taught his disciples through His own conduct and precepts. Shri Sai Satcharitra amply elaborates on this universalism of Baba in the backdrop of some day-to-day happenings at Shirdi. Following the Master, Sai devotees should, therefore, develop the highest quality of religious tolerance. As Baba used to say all are the children of God and He is the only and ultimate Lord.

New Year Message 2005

Shri Sai Baba of Shirdi is verily called as Sadguru, Fakir, Awalia, Maha Yogi and most importantly "the Incarnation of the Age". During the stay of Baba at Shirdi some spiritual personalities used to pay visit to that place.

Once, on seeing Baba as a young person at Shirdi one such personality Shri Gangagir commented that the young Sai was like a jewel under a heap of cow-dung and also that one day His divine illumination will bring glory to Shirdi.

Meher Baba, a disciple of Upasani Maharaj (who was the Prime disciple of Baba) has commented that Shri Sai is like the beginning and end of creation. Upasani Maharaj has spoken a lot on Shri Sai, saying that Shri Sai is the Satchidananda God.

Thus, a lot has been spoken and written on Shri Sai. Hundreds of epithets have been used in His name. The "Sai Nam Astottarasata Namahvalih" (108 names of Baba) glorifying the names and divine qualifies of Shri Sai are recited in most of the Sai temples. People during His time and as also today have exhaustively written on this majestic and unfathomable divine personality, the past and present miraculous deeds related to Him and on the emotional attachment of the devotees with Him. Crores of people have been drawn towards Him and thousands of temples have been built all over India and some in other countries in His name. His photographs and paintings can be seen everywhere temples, houses, shops, vehicles. The process of such expansion continues. Today He is the Sai - the Master and father to so many. The number of devotees is ever on the increase and this "Sai Wave" is slowly but surely engulfing humanity.

Speculations apart, fact remains that the divine status of Shri Sai has not been exactly defined as yet. The Hindus use all terminologies and epithets quoting from their scriptures to explain the divine attributes and Leelas of Shri Sai. Thus Shri Sai is worshipped as Sai Maharai, Sai Bhagwan, Sai -Ram, Sai Krishna, Sai Vithala, Sai-Mauli (means mother), Sai Param Brahma, Sai Shiva, Sai Dattatreya, Sai Vishnoo, Sai Shankara, Sai Avatara, Sai Ishwara, and Sai Ganesha etc. Would one analyse these divine epithets He would be drawn to the conclusion that although Shri Sai Baba played the role of a Sadguru i.e. a Perfect Master while at Shirdi, He is much beyond that. Shri Sai left His human embodiment long time ago, without institutionalizing his movement and without leaving an heir-apparent as most of the Gurus do. He came to serve His devotees for their spiritual evolution, although He also rendered temporal benefit to all of them through His kind words and kinder actions. An analysis of the visible personality of Shri Sai would indicate that he was totally detached from all material needs, was sometimes in a Jalali (spiritually intoxicated) state, used his spiritual powers for the benefit of his devotees in abundance, treated all equally not-withstanding the differentiations of caste, religion, creed, language, temporal status, etc.; was divinely compassionate to all, including animals. Although He was a God-realized soul yet He behaved like an ordinary man in a village without any assertions of His divine hierarchy (as many Gurus do). He lived in one place for sixty years and left His body having served who-so--ever came to Him without seeking any returns.

Today Shri Sai is a name known to most of the people of India. Shirdi has become a 'Tirath' with devotees from all over the world making a bee-line there. The "Saism" as many call it, is expanding very fast. Such expansion by sheer self- motivation of His devotees indicates the power that "Shri Sai" is even eighty six years after His Samadhi. This is what happened to all the incarnations in the past.

Let us pray to Shri Sai, "the Incarnation of the Age" on the New Years' day to guide and bless us.

Dussehra Message 2004

An in-depth analysis of the Path shown by Baba leads to certain obvious pointers essentially required for spiritual evolution of human beings. Baba, during His interaction with a very large number of devotees of different religions and paths had repeatedly brought out certain common emotional, psychological and physical parameters to be followed by the devotees. Although specific instructions were given directly or indirectly to most of the devotees to solve their immediate or mundane problems, yet the general parameters for ethical living and spiritual evolution were more profound and long termed. After Baba left His human form, those who followed the parameters and advice for the rest of their lives benefited immensely. Others, who deviated, in the absence of interaction with the Sadguru, did not evolve much. This is the conclusion one is bound to draw when lives of the prominent devotees of Baba are examined as a whole.

These general parameters for a contented and evolved life have been brought to the fore extensively in Shri Sai Satcharitra when it narrates devotees' real-life happenings at Shirdi, as also the anecdotes and interpretations pertaining Shri Sai Baba. Most of the other books written on Baba have also tried to bring out these parameters in different ways. Thus for a good disciple the examples/anecdotes from the life of Baba and his percepts, as codified in Shri Sai Satcharitra and other published materials should work as the best reference points of guidance for their ethical conduct and spiritual progress. This is why I always prescribe reading of Shri Sai Satcharitra in particular and other related materials to the devotees and others following any path or religion. Whenever in doubt about his thoughts and actions a devotee should try to relate these with the informations on similar situations provided in Shri Sai Satcharitra. He should always evaluate to find out as to how far he is able to progress with reference to these parameters as the permanent principles of an ethical existence.

Baba has spoken about the loftiest principles in the simplest way, when exemplifying these principles through his own conduct as well. For example let us take the case of a man who spoke ill of another devotee to Baba when He was returning from Lendi Bagh. This finds a mention in chapter 18-19 of the Shri Sai Satcharitra. Baba told him that pigs will only eat dirt even if they are given the best of food. The meaning of this sentence is too obvious to be explained. Or when, while giving two rupees to a person who had helped Baba with a step ladder in going up and coming down the home of Radhakrishnamayi, Baba announced that one must pay for the labour rendered by any person. In fact the entire gamut of all his advice reiterates the principles of ethical conduct reflected in Shrimad Bhagavata Gita.

The problem with some of the devotees is that they read Shri Sai Satcharitra more intensely for its stories depicting miracles rather than for understanding the applied principles of ethical living as prescribed by Baba. Further while carrying on their mundane deeds or misdeeds they often forget Baba's advice at that moment. Therefore, they are prone to ask the same questions on various issues again and again over the years when ever in trouble. What Baba wanted the followers to do is more to practice these principles than only to read. As Baba's intentions reveal, the question is not as to how many times one has failed while trying but as to whether he is determined and remembers to apply these principles while doing any act, good or bad. Each devotee needs to ask this question to himself and find the answer. Shri Sai Satcharitra can only give them guidelines.

Guru Purnima Message 2004

Some people view and see scientific knowledge as a method of understanding the different laws of nature with a view to control and apply these for the benefit of the human race and others. They view the scientific discoveries, inventions, newer technologies from intellectual, empirical and utilitarian points of view which can be cognized directly through the cognitive faculties like the eyes and ears and indirectly through artifacts created by them (for example: a radio, transistor transmitting electronic waves). Whereas this is not contradicted, there are very few people who interconnect their rational approach with the spiritual approach pursued by some other people. These two separate approaches if not looked at in a holistic manner, lead to certain contradictions. The purely spiritual group says that there is a God who cannot be seen and proved in the manner in which scientific evidences are established but He can only be experienced through subtle inner perceptions. On the other hand, the purely scientific groups argue that but for scientific evidence, the so called God, his mythological concepts and miracles cannot be accepted. These two approaches at the extreme end would have rendered the human civilization apart had not the majority of humanity believed in the existence of a supernatural power called God, Allah, nature or called by whatever name. On this world of ours, though human societies have changed, their economic and political factors have changed, yet the concept of God has never changed. For the Hindus, Ram remains Ram, for the Christians, Christ remains Christ and for the Muslims, Prophet Mohamed remains Prophet Mohamed, notwithstanding, the fact that societies propounding such faiths have undergone vast economic, social and political changes over the time.

All such thoughts bring to mind a fundamental question - can there be a God who has created two unrelated and independent principles- scientific principles and the spiritual principles? Is it that scientific principles, like the discoveries and technology created by the human brain, are a mere chance occurrence in the gradual process of evolution or can they be viewed from a spiritualistic angle or vision? Yesterday, when Einstein expounded his theory on inter-connectivity between matter and energy in his famous formula, $E=MC^2$ he tried to explain the entire universe through this single equation. He could not however, succeed because he could not contemplate the interconnectivity between consciousness, energy and matter. Nevertheless, Einstein was a genius and he did acknowledge that he experienced an infinite subtle world much beyond the perceptible matter and energy world which he was unable to explain. In other words, Einstein, the great scientist experienced and had the intellectual honesty to express his limitations about the subtle energy field existing in the world beyond. Had a genius like Einstein gone a little ahead and approached the issue from a different angle as has been explained in many spiritual books like the Gita and the Bible, he could, perhaps, have been able to connect the apparently diversified theorems into a single formulation. Had he got the sixth sense of the spiritual practitioners and saints, he could have unearthed more about the subtle forms of the universe and nature. If Einstein is taken as a model, it means that it is possible for the scientific-oriented minds to have a different approach towards the unearthing of the mysteries of nature in the manner followed by the great seers of various religions. But rarely have human beings come across such great personalities like Aryabhatta of India, Pythagoras of the ancient Greece. When the Spiritual Masters in different forms gave a spiritual thrust to the nascent human civilization, they obviously did not jump steps and straightaway start teaching theology and philosophy. At the earliest stages what they did was to generate certain types of logic in the human minds without which it would not have been possible for them to pick up the complex and finer aspects of nature. Hence, the simple logic generated in the minds of human beings were evolved to grow more complex logic at later stages. What they taught was simple arithmetic (relating to numbers) and geometry (relating to shapes) and out of this mathematics, other branches of science developed. Through these symbols they could explain the different phenomena of the vast world of nature more easily. At the second stage they gave the concepts of architectural designs, and simple mathematical calculations, etc. Like a newborn child looking at the world around with a surprised look, the human race started picking these concepts up rather anxiously. Once they were ready, their brain cells were geared to make higher scientific discoveries, etc. through the use of this logic. A few individuals who were ready for it were then systematically given the required thought process and it is these individuals who propounded the theories of science like Marconi's Law of Radio waves, Newton's Law of Gravity or Einstein's Law of Relativity.

Today, such discoveries and the related technology have gone to great extents like conquering the space, cloning, genetic engineering, etc. which yesterday if done by any human being would have been construed as a divine act. Logically, therefore the secrets of nature are being revealed to the human beings with a purpose of expanding the horizons of their knowledge through the expansion of the brain capacity. Given this background, it is evident that the very basis of scientific thought has emanated out of the thrust given by these spiritual beings who had incarnated on this globe with a superior intelligence. Obviously, when the living creatures of earth had not experienced subtle thought processes some souls coming from outside stirred them. These superior beings must have carried such superior intelligence from their evolution in past lives. Commonly defined as transcendental intelligence, such intellects could not have achieved such levels of excellence in a single life time. The inspirational revelations of many spiritual personalities holding such transcendental intelligence on this solar system (of which earth forms a part) is a near probability. Today in scientific literature, we can well see the imaginative depiction of such characters/events as inter stellar warfare, UFOs, etc. The present fourth human civilization is on the threshold of transcending to the fifth human race. More and more scientific discoveries and experimentations will be undertaken by a few generations of human beings and this will create a group which will have the potentiality of controlling the subtle forces of nature without the help of artifacts. That is, as the time progresses ahead, they will depend more and more on their inner faculties of mind to capture and use the subtler forces of nature than to depend on the machines created by them. For example, they will communicate with each other through the subtle faculties of their brain, rather than using a telephone or a cell phone. The sixth sense of the intellectual faculty is bound to expand much more than it is today. This will force human society to look at the world of religion and the world of science from a totally different perspective. That perspective is to find the root principles from which both scientific approach and religious approach evolved and establish their interconnectivity. Thus if the contradictions between the two approaches can be reconciled then the benefit of science and technology shall not be used for destructive purposes. It would be coloured through the spiritual approach of kindness and tolerance.

Ram Navami Message 2004

Some people believe in vegetarianism which means avoidance of consumption of the flesh of any species their eggs or any direct by-product. They limit their food to vegetables, fruits, other agricultural products, milk and milk products of different animals. Some of them go to the extent of even avoiding brinjals, onions, garlics, etc. considering them to be as harmful as non-vegetarian products. By some people are stated to be non-vegetarian in nature. Strangely, these people take milk of animals considering it to be vegetarian food. Here is a situation in which one is to believe that onion is not the outcome of a vegetarian plant like banana but the product of an organic body like an egg laid by a hen.

Non-vegetarians believe in eating the flesh of some species, their milk, eggs of birds, etc. Whereas some people claim themselves to be purely vegetarian in food habits, non-vegetarians can never call themselves purely non-vegetarian, since they also take fruits, vegetables and milk etc. Neither any non-vegetarian nor for that purpose any vegetarian person can be said to be pure in the true sense of the term. Food items like cakes, biscuits and many other products available in the market, certain medicines, tonics etc. contain -different enzymes and materials from non-human species, as do many of the items that we use on a day to day basis, like creams and soaps which contain animal's fats etc. The vegetarian group belonging to the so called intellectual class of society is fully aware of the inclusion of non-vegetarian elements in the so called harmless vegetarian items. Yet they take these items beholding some traditional or acquired value of vegetarianism. This has always been the case with the intellectual group. It is expediency which justifies every thing. Taking out milk from the mouth of a calf and yet worshipping the cow as a mother is justified on the grounds of expediency. It is expediency which forces the human society to create hybrid varieties of -different species of animals and birds ultimately to eat them like chicken or put them into different uses. Most of the demonstrative compassion shown towards animals, birds and other species comes out of this utilitarian mindset of the homo sapiens. The highest compassion to other species in the recorded history of mankind was shown by Mahavira Jain, but how many people understand it and follow it in the right spirit.

Whatever be the justification in killing the members of other species, the mute question is "Does anyone wishes to be killed?" Does any human being wish to be killed and eaten by any other species except in cases of rare psychological predispositions like suicide etc. Will any hen or goat when asked say that it wants to be killed? Have we not observed the pain and terror in the eyes and tremor in the bodies of the animals and birds when they are being slaughtered? When the very man who does not want to be killed at any cost or even to be injured kills an animal, is he not being totally insensitive to the pain of others? This logically justifies the theory that the strong rule or have a moral right to rule and exploit the weak. This is true in the animal world where instinctively the tiger kills the deer as intelligence has not developed in it as in human beings. Once its hunger is quenched, it kills no more till hunger proples it, instinctively again, to kill a prey. The human species, on the other hand, even keep a stock of flesh of dead animals in packed or frozen condition for eating whenever it likes.

The word 'Humanism' (Manav-vada) used by the so called civilised society explains an attitude/act of kindness and understanding towards other human beings to whatever breed they belong. The word 'Manav-vada' does not necessarily include 'Prani-vada'. And this is where the human society falters. The urge to kill animals when further extended as a psychological condition can lead a person to kill other human beings and strengthens the mental trait of violence. Have not we observed that even today human beings are, at times, cruelly killed by other human beings in the manner in which an animal is killed by another animal. Have we not read that in the places where the sages and saints lived, even animals lost their cruel instincts. Why? Because of the non-existence of killer mindset and an attitude of peaceful co-existence of different species. Can't the human species create an atmosphere of peaceful co-existence with the animals. Has not God provided us with enough of agricultural products, fruits, roots, etc. on which human society can subsist!

The question is left open to the reader to decide for himself rationally even if not from the religious or spiritual points of view. A non-vegetarian person may not personally kill or be a part of the process of killing, but he certainly contributes to such killings as a consumer. To appreciate the issue properly, it would perhaps be better for a non-vegetarian person to visit a place where animals/birds are being killed, observe the painful reactions of these harmless species when death is being inflicted on them and then decide whether he should continue to be a non-vegetarian.

The direct experience of things (and not information alone) brings knowledge and creates a conviction whether to do or not do a thing. A progressive man should have direct experience and then decide on the course of action he likes to take. This is truthful living and without truthful living one cannot enter into the path of spiritualism.

New Year Message 2004

Devotees speak volumes about their Masters. They speak on the Master's glory, personality, activities, miracles, their personal experiences, and of other devotees with the Masters and their group activities etc. Particularly, when it comes to Shri Sainath Maharaj, devotees speak more about dreams with relation to Him, their own experience which they call miracles and on their inner and emotive communications with Baba. In short, they experience Him as a Personal God, who can be a Sadguru or a deity. Some of them worship a number of Personal Gods at the same time and therefore, find it difficult to focus on one. In any case the One and the Ultimate God the Almighty has to be beyond all the Personal Gods. A Personal God, by whatever name, is called Saguna (with certain qualities and powers) Sakara (with a form which a human mind can ordinarily comprehend). A finer understanding of God is Nirguna (beyond such limited qualities and powers), Nirakara (beyond all form). Nirguna Nirakara - this means seeing or experiencing the essence of God or that Ultimate reality or Brahma in all its creations, i.e., in the devotee himself and in the entire manifested and non-manifested creation around him.

By this logic all statues or paintings, structures (like Samadhis), names, Aartis, Mantras, Charan Padukas, etc. are symbols of God and certainly not God, the Ultimate. Such symbols are generally worshipped and contemplated on as it is easy for the limited human mind to comprehend them. The question is whether the human mind should necessarily be limited, or a path should be chosen to keep it limited. If any path or any religion prescribes such an approach, it itself is limited. Hinduism prescribes certain methods by which a devotee can graduate from a Sakara (limited form) of worship to a

Nirakara (form-less) worship. Religion means both ritualism and spiritualism. Unless one transcends ritualism, it is difficult to enter into the arena of spiritualism in the true sense of the term. Spiritualism means to follow the true diktats of the spirit within. Generally speaking, 'the spirit within' means the soul, which is a part of that God, the Ultimate who encompasses both the seen and unseen, the living and non-living aspects of nature and from the smallest particles to biggest stars. Spiritualism, therefore, has necessarily to expand the spirit of the soul from its limited body-bounden awareness to a vast cosmic awareness. If sheer ritualisms like Puja, Archana, Yagyans do not uplih the spirit of the individual or expand his mental horizon, it certainly is not spiritualism.

Generally, it is due to the lack of understanding of what real spiritualism means that most of the devotees spend their whole life doing certain rituals without progressing. From multiple forms of God to a single form God to a formless state of God is the real prescription for spiritualism. Multiple form worships (i.e. of deities etc.) do not give focus on a particular form. Since these various symbolic representations of different aspects of nature go with various functions and powers, a person worshipping these forms gets scared to stop such worship even when he understands that he has to graduate to a formless state of worship. For example, Shri Ganapati is for the removal of obstructions, Shri Durga is for protection against enemies or Shri Laxmi is for prosperity or Shri Hanumana for courage, etc. No doubt that all the four deities are manifestations of the Ultimate One but then on whom does the devotee concentrate? Where then is the question of what is called "Ekagra Chitta" as a sine-qua-non for subtle experience of God. In such a situation one has to choose one of the two ways. Either to worship the Ultimate One (Nirguna Nirakara) going beyond the worship of these deities or to evolve through these limited forms to the Ultimate reality through Gyana Marga (Path of Knowledge). All spiritual practitioners in all ages, of whichever religion, have gone through this process of leaving the forms and contemplating on the formless state of God or in experiencing the formless state of God through the forms. The Perfect Masters or Sadgurus always taught the same method to their disciples at a certain stage of evolution. Those who followed them and tried to experience the impersonal aspects of God evolved faster than those that stuck on to the Personal aspect of God only. Thus Baba has clearly stated in Shri Sai Satcharitra that the best way of worship is to experience Him as a Formless, Universal existence. If not, to worship Him with a form. Therefore, the devotee of Baba while worshipping Him with a form, should always try to experience Him as the formless. But then, the big question is how to be focused and be in a state of "Ekagra Chitta" when too many forms are contemplated on at the same time. Is not the form of the Sadguru enough!

Glossary

The Glossary enlists briefly the non-English terms used in the text of this book that call for clarification of their meaning and usage.

The spellings of non-English terms are derived from Sanskrit, Hindi and Urdu, and they are neither phonetic nor based on a specific scheme of Romanization.

Aarti – Prayer performed with lighted lamps, etc.

Abhimana - pride

Ajapa jaap – effortless, continuous and natural repetition of God's name with every breadth

Ankita Santana – chosen child of God

Aasans – Yogic and meditative postures

Atma – the soul

Avtaar – the manifestation of God in human form on earth; the direct descent of Reality into illusion; the Saviour

Bhava – mental attitude; emotion; mood

Bhajan – devotional song

Bhakti - Devotion

Bhakti Marg – path of devotion

Brahma- the Creator of universe

Chillum – clay pipe for smoking

Darshan – to get an audience/meeting

Dharma – Righteousness; rules or conduct of balanced sustenance

Dhuni – sacred fire

Ghat – living body

Guru- the Master, Spiritual Master

Guru Kripa – grace of the Master

Jaap – repetitive chanting

Jiva – *human soul*

Jivanmukta – beyond the cycle of birth and death

Jeetejee marna - dying while living

Kalas – type of power

Karma – action; effects; natural happenings preconditioned by one's past lives

Karmik – caused by or effect of a person's actions; destiny

Kundalini – vital energy force, primordial energy force

Manasa jaap – mentally repeating or chanting God's Name

Maya – worldly illusion

Mantra – religious verses having spiritual-occult potentiality or a set of words in a particular configuration and rhythm repeated in prayer or meditation

Mukti - liberation

Naam jaap- chanting of God's name

naam smarana – remembrance of the name of God

Naivedya – offering to the worshipped One

Navadha Bhaktis - nine methods of expression of devotion

Nirakara – formless

Paap – misdeed; a wrongful act

Panchopachar- Five elements

Paramhansa – beyond limits of nature

Parampara - tradition

Parayan – devotional reading of sacred text

Parmatma – the Oversoul; Universal soul; Almighty God

Parashakti - Primordial energy form of the universe

Pooja – prayer; act of devotion

Prana - vital force

Praan Pratishtha – consecration

Pranayam – breath controlling exercises

Prarabdha – the inevitable destiny of each lifetime; the impressions from the past lives that determine destiny

Prashad – distribution of the offering made to the Lord

Punya – a pious act, virtue

Rinanubandha - the payment made by human beings to settle debts of past lives

Saburi - patience

Sadgati – liberation of soul from cycle of birth and death

Sadguru – Perfect Master

Sadhana – practice; endeavour; directing towards the goal

Sakara – form of God

Sakha - friend

Samadhi – the place where a holy person is laid to rest

Samashti – group

Samskara – impressions; imprints of the past experiences

Satsang – company of the pious and devotional people

Shishya - disciple

Shraddha – devotional faith

Siddha – one who has attained perfection; Adept

Siddhi – mystic power; occult power

Swabhimana – self respect

Swaroop - form

Vedas – Knowledge, ancient scriptures of Hinduism

Vyasthi - individual

Yoga – yoking; disciplined activity to realize union with God

Yogi – one who practices yoga

Our books on Shirdi Sai Baba

ShirdiSaiBabaisahouseholdnameinIndia
aswellasinmanypartsoftheworldtoday .
Thesebooksof ferfascinatingglimpsesinto
thelifeandmiraclesofShirdiSaiBabaand
otherPerfectMasters. Thesebookswill
provideyouwithanexperiencethatisbound
totransformone'ssenseofperspectiveand
bringaboutperceptibleandmeaningful
spiritualgrowth.

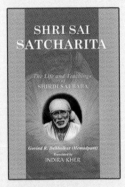

SHRISAISA TCHARITA
TheLifeand Teachings of
ShirdiSaiBaba
TranslatedbyIndiraKher
ISBN 81207 22116 Rs.500(HB)
ISBN 81207 21535 Rs. 300(PB)

BABA-MayI Answer
C.B.Satpathy
ISBN9788120745940
Rs.150

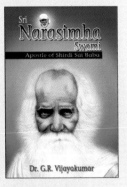

SriNarasimhaSwami
ApostleofShirdiSaiBaba
Dr.G.R.V ijayakumar
ISBN9788120744325
Rs. 90

Baba'sV aani:HisSayings
and Teachings
CompiledbyV innyChitluri
ISBN9788120738591Rs.200

SpotlightontheSaiStory
Chakor Ajgaonker
ISBN8120743991   Rs.200

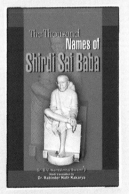

The ThousandNamesof
ShirdiSaiBaba
SriB.V .NarasimhaSwamiJi
ISBN9788120737389Rs.75

ShirdiSaiBabaand
OtherPerfectMasters
CBSatpathy
ISBN978 81207 23848 Rs.135

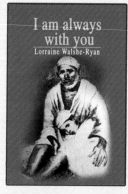

Iamalwayswithyou
LorraineW alshe-Ryan
ISBN 8120731929 Rs.150

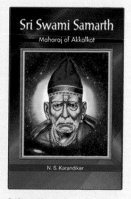

SriSwamiSamarth–
Maharajof Akkalkot
N.S.Karandikar
ISBN9788120734456 Rs.200

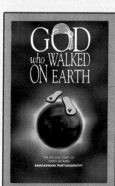

GodWhoW alkedonEarth:
TheLife& Times
ofShirdiSaiBaba
RParthasarathy
ISBN8120718097 Rs.95

Baba'sR inanubandh:
Leelasd uringH is Sojourn
in Shirdi
Compiledb yV innyC hitluri
ISBN81 20 73 4036 R s. 200

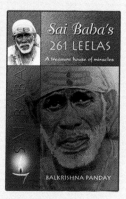

SaiBaba' s261Leelas
BalkrishnaPanday
ISBN8120727274Rs.75

108NamesofShirdiSaiBaba
ISBN8120730748
Rs.50

UnravellingtheEnigma
MarrianneW arren
ISBN8120721470 Rs.400

GuruCharitra
ShreeSwamiSamarth
ISBN9788120733480 Rs.200

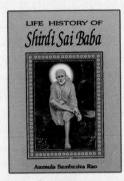

LifeHistoryofShirdiSai Baba
AmmulaSambasivaRao
ISBN8120720334
Rs.95

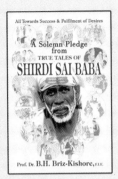

AS olemnP ledge
from True Tales of Shirdi Sai Baba
Dr BH B riz-Kishore
ISBN8 12 072 240x
Rs. 95(Alsoa vailablei nH indi,
Tamil, Kannada& Telugu)

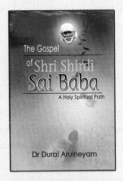

The Gospelo f ShriS hirdi Sai Baba:
AHolySpiritualPath
DrDurai Arulneyam
ISBN9788120739970
Rs.150

ShriShirdiSaiBaba:His
LifeandMiracles
ISBN8120728777Rs.25

ShriSaiBaba' sTeachings&
Philosophy
LtColMBNimbalkar
ISBN8120723643Rs.75

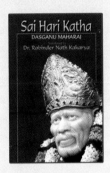

SaiHariKatha
DasganuMaharaj
ISBN9788120733244
Rs.75

SaiBaba:HisDivineGlimpses
VBKher
ISBN8120722914Rs.95

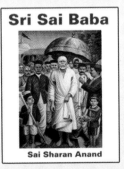

SriSaiBaba
SaiSharan Anand
ISBN8120719506Rs.125

ShirdiSaiSpeaks...
SabKaMalikEk
QuotesfortheDay
ISBN8120731018Rs.200
(AlsoavailableinHindi)

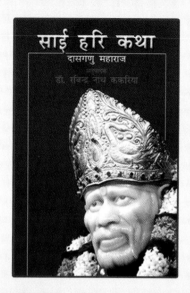

साईहरिकथा
दासगणुमहाराज
ISBN 9788120733237   Rs.65

साई—सबकामालिक
कल्पनाभाकुनी
ISBN9788120733206Rs.100

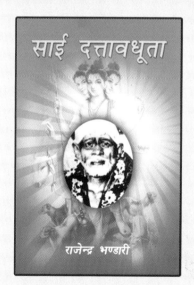

साईदत्तावधूता
राजेन्द्रभण्डारी
ISBN8120744041Rs.75

श्रीशिरडीसाईबाबावअन्यसद्गुरु
चन्द्रभानुसतपथी
ISBN8120744011Rs.90

श्रीसाईसच्चरित्रा
डॉरबिन्द्रनाथककरिया
ISBN 8120725018   Rs. 250 (PB)
ISBN812072500XRs.   300 (HB)

साईशरणमें
चन्द्रभानुसतपथी
ISBN8120728025Rs.   100

पृथ्वी पर अवतरित भगवान
शिरड़ी के साई बाबा
रंगास्वामी पार्थसारथी
ISBN8 12 072 1012   Rs. 95

श्रीसाईबाबाकेपरमभक्त
डॉरबिन्द्रनाथककरिया
ISBN8120727797   Rs. 75

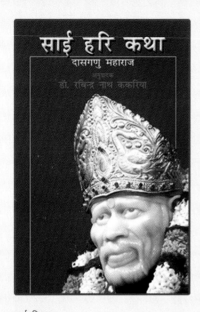

साईहरिकथा
दासगणुमहाराज
ISBN 9788120733237   Rs.65

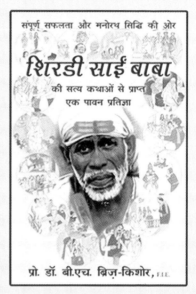

शिरडीसाईबाबा
प्रोडॉबीएचब्रिज़-किशोर
ISBN8120723465   Rs.60

साईकासंदेश
डॉरबिन्द्रनाथककरिया
ISBN8120728793Rs.   90

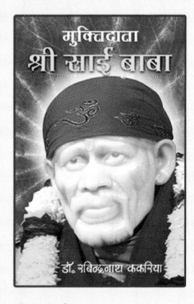

मुक्तिदाताश्रीसाईबाबा
डॉरबिन्द्रनाथककरिया
ISBN812072778   9 Rs. 60

साईभक्तानुभव
डॉ.रबिन्द्रनाथककरिया
ISBN 9788120730526   Rs. 90

श्रीसाईबाबाकेअनन्यभक्त
डॉरबिन्द्रनाथककरिया
ISBN 8120727053Rs.   75

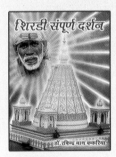

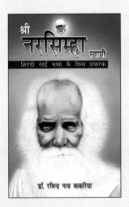

शिरडीसंपूर्णदर्शन
डॉरबिन्द्रनाथककरिया
ISBN8120723120   Rs. 50

शिरडीसाईकेदिव्यवचन
सबकामालिकएक
ISBN9788120735330   Rs.180

श्रीनरसिम्हास्वामी
शिरडीसाईबाबाकेदिव्यप्रचारक
डॉरबिन्द्रनाथककरिया
ISBN 9788120744370
Rs.75

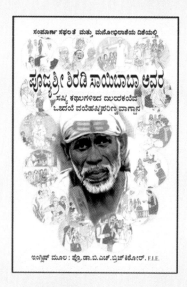

ShirdiSaiBaba(Kannada)
Prof.Dr .B.H.BrizKishore
ISBN8120728734   Rs.60

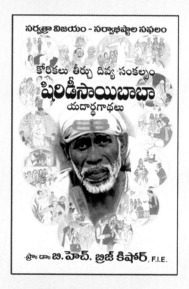

ShirdiSaiBaba(T elugu)
Prof.Dr .B.H.BrizKishore
ISBN8120722949   Rs.60

ShirdiSaiBaba(T amil)
Prof.Dr .B.H.BrizKishore
ISBN8120728769   Rs.60